# How To Be A Lawyer's Client

Ray Birkinsha

**How To Be A Lawyer's Client**
By Ray Birkinsha

Ray Birkinsha
DBA/MileStones Press
West Bloomfield, MI
ray@milestonespress.com

Copyright © 2012
All rights reserved. No part of this book may be reproduced or transmitted in any form or by any means, electronic or mechanical, including photocopying, recording or any information storage and retrieval system, without written permission from the author

ISBN-13: 978-1479301317
ISBN-10: 1479301310
First Edition
Printed in the United States of America

# Table of Contents

1. **Introduction** --------------------------------------------------------- 1
   1.1  Why Use A Lawyer? ----------------------------------------- 1
   1.2  What This Book Is about and How It's Organized ---------- 3
   1.3  How This Book Can Help You ----------------------------------- 4
   1.4  How This Book Will Probably not Help You ------------------ 7
   1.5  The Important Legal Disclaimer ------------------------------ 8

2. **Becoming a Lawyer** ------------------------------------------ 10
   2.1  Education --------------------------------------------------------- 11
   2.2  The Bar Exam ---------------------------------------------------- 13
   2.3  Admission to Practice Law ----------------------------------- 16
   2.4  Representing Clients ------------------------------------------ 17
   2.5  The Law Firm ---------------------------------------------------- 19
   2.6  Continuing Legal Education and Accomplishments ------- 21

3. **Types of Law and Expertise** ---------------------------------- 23
   3.1  A Very Short History of the Law ----------------------------- 23
   3.2  Types of Law ----------------------------------------------------- 25
   3.3  How Lawyers Specialize --------------------------------------- 26
   3.4  Measuring Expertise ------------------------------------------- 28

4. **How to Find Your Lawyer** ------------------------------------- 29
   4.1  Law Firms --------------------------------------------------------- 29
   4.2  What You Should Be Looking for ----------------------------- 33
   4.3  Identifying the Expertise You Need ------------------------- 35
   4.4  How to Find a Lawyer ------------------------------------------ 37
   4.5  The Interview: What to Ask ---------------------------------- 40
   4.6  The Interview—How to Ask ----------------------------------- 43
   4.7  Lawyers to Avoid ------------------------------------------------ 45
   4.8  Making a Decision ---------------------------------------------- 46

5. **The Lawyer's Fee—How You Pay** ---------------------------- 48
   5.1  Financial Advantage? ------------------------------------------ 48
   5.2  Set Expectations ------------------------------------------------ 49
   5.3  The Hourly Fee -------------------------------------------------- 51
   5.4  The Contingency Fee ------------------------------------------ 52
   5.5  The Retainer ----------------------------------------------------- 55
   5.6  The Fixed Fee --------------------------------------------------- 56
   5.7  Things to Remember ------------------------------------------- 57

i

| | | |
|---|---|---|
| **6.** | **The Professional Relationship** | **59** |
| 6.1 | The Attorney-Client Relationship | 59 |
| 6.2 | What Your Lawyer Expects from You | 62 |
| 6.3 | The Rules of Ethics | 64 |
| 6.4 | What the Ethical Lawyer Can't Do | 66 |
| 6.5 | The Insurance Defense Lawyer | 68 |
| 6.6 | The Lawyer's Ethical Obligations | 69 |
| **7.** | **The Lawyer's Job** | **70** |
| 7.1 | What the Lawyer Does Every Day | 70 |
| 7.2 | Leave It to the Professional | 74 |
| 7.3 | How to Help Your Lawyer | 75 |
| 7.4 | Malpractice | 76 |
| **8.** | **Your Responsibility** | **78** |
| 8.1 | Decisions | 78 |
| 8.2 | Be Aware | 79 |
| 8.3 | Document Communication | 80 |
| 8.4 | Be Organized | 81 |
| 8.5 | Make the Tough Decisions | 82 |
| **9.** | **Civil Litigation** | **88** |
| 9.1 | Civil Courts | 88 |
| 9.2 | Rules and Procedures | 90 |
| 9.3 | Beginning the Lawsuit | 90 |
| 9.4 | Pleadings and Motions | 92 |
| 9.5 | Parties | 96 |
| 9.6 | Depositions and Discovery | 98 |
| 9.7 | Trials | 102 |
| 9.8 | Judgments | 114 |
| 9.9 | Appeals | 115 |
| 9.10 | Remedies | 118 |
| 9.11 | Resolution | 120 |
| 9.12 | Verdict | 124 |
| **10.** | **Criminal Litigation** | **126** |
| 10.1 | Overview | 126 |
| 10.2 | Rules and Procedure | 127 |
| 10.3 | Preliminary Proceedings | 127 |
| 10.4 | Preparation for Trial | 130 |
| 10.5 | Trial | 132 |
| 10.6 | Appeals | 138 |
| 10.7 | Resolution | 140 |

| | | |
|---|---|---|
| **11.** | **Organizing Your Litigation** | **142** |
| 11.1 | What to Keep | 142 |
| 11.2 | How to Organize Your Documents | 145 |
| 11.3 | Electronic Organization | 148 |
| 11.4 | Your Working File | 151 |
| 11.5 | After the Case Ends | 152 |
| **12.** | **The Most Common Problems** | **153** |
| 12.1 | Communication | 154 |
| 12.2 | Control | 160 |
| 12.3 | Fee Disputes | 164 |
| 12.4 | The Wrong Result | 168 |
| 12.5 | Malpractice | 173 |
| 12.6 | Discovering Malpractice. | 176 |
| **13.** | **Resolving Problems** | **178** |
| 13.1 | Communicate | 178 |
| 13.2 | Replacing Your Lawyer | 180 |
| 13.3 | Bar Complaints | 184 |
| 13.4 | Suing Your Lawyer | 186 |
| **14.** | **Conclusion** | **190** |
| **15.** | **Sample Letters and Forms** | **198** |
| 15.1 | Interview Outline | 198 |
| 15.2 | Engagement Letter | 200 |
| 15.3 | Confirming Conversations and Decisions | 202 |
| 15.4 | Status Report Outline | 204 |
| 15.5 | Complaint/Issue Letter | 205 |
| 15.6 | Replacement Letter | 206 |
| **16** | **Sample Jury Instructions** | **207** |

Dedicated to Michelle in appreciation for her support and her love – and forcing me to finish this book!

With gratitude to our families.

# 1. Introduction

*If it weren't for lawyers, we wouldn't need them.*

## 1.1 Why Use A Lawyer?

Every year people find themselves needing legal advice or requiring representation in a court proceeding. They may be going through a divorce, being sued for breaking a promise, charged with a criminal act, or needing a lawyer to represent them after being injured by someone else. While these legal problems are different, they have things in common. No matter what the circumstances, becoming involved in the American legal system for the first time can be stressful. For most people the legal arena is a very different world and one where they have to deal with some of the most intimidating professionals in the country—lawyers.

So why hire a lawyer? There are good reasons that most people involved in a legal issue should hire a lawyer. The most basic one is that the law and the legal system are complicated. When hiring a lawyer, you're looking for someone with knowledge of the law. Lawyers are trained for years to understand not only the basics of the legal system, but how to find and understand the law as it might apply to a specific problem. A good lawyer has years of experience in handling specific kinds of cases like personal injury, divorces, or business contracts, and has also developed the ability to efficiently research the law and figure out what it means to his or her clients.

Some people are willing to spend time and do the work to represent themselves in a legal issue. With all of the resources available today, it's possible to gain a basic understanding of a specific area of the law. The problem with representing yourself is that it's very hard to learn the nuances of the law, and almost impossible to learn how the court system operates from a book or website.

Understanding how the courts work really takes two different kinds of knowledge. The first is an understanding of the formal rules the courts follow. The second is knowing how individual courts—and specific judges—really operate. That comes from experience working with judges in a specific legal jurisdiction.

The formal rules and procedures of our judicial system are complicated on paper, but in practice, they can be even more complicated. Judges have a great deal of discretion in how they apply these rules. Sometimes they're applied just like they're written, but what usually happens is that each county or city—and sometimes individual judges—develop their own methods for handling cases and the lawyers they work with. People who represent themselves can run into trouble when they fail to appreciate both the formal requirements *and* the traditions and processes of the local courts.

Chapters 9 and 10 are designed to give you a broad overview of how our courts work. They will help you talk to and understand your lawyer when he discusses how your case or litigation is proceeding. This material is *not* designed to allow you to navigate the court system on your own.

Another important reason you may hire a lawyer is because of his or her knowledge of the people involved in your legal problem. Depending on the nature of your problem, it may be very important to know the lawyers who represent the other side, the political figures involved or the experts who may be needed to present or support your position. In really big cities, this insider knowledge may not be as big an issue with run-of-the-mill cases, but even in the large metro areas, the better lawyers know each other and have worked together in the past. Like any other profession, being successful is usually a combination of what you know and who you know.

The last reason to hire a lawyer is to take advantage of the skills and abilities they've developed over years of practicing law. Depending on the nature of your legal issue, the skill you need could be legal writing, public speaking, negotiation, not being intimidated by an aggressive opponent, or the ability to solve legal problems. These skills are developed over time through daily practice in the legal system.

For example, most of us would eventually become used to speaking on our own behalf to a judge or a jury if we did it every day for several years. But if we're suddenly forced to participate in a legal proceeding where we are not comfortable, we may stumble and even be terrified. A good lawyer, on the other hand, has had this kind of practice.

Years ago I represented a client and sued a defendant who represented himself. My client believed he was owed money and the defendant believed he didn't owe it. The defendant was articulate and intelligent—a born salesman—and was convinced he knew the law and the facts. But when we appeared in front of the judge, he was unable to organize his arguments. He was unfamiliar with the legal questions the judge asked. He quickly became frustrated, making it hard for him to speak. I'm sure that with the right education and experience, he could have represented himself, but it was a new experience for him, so he didn't do well. The legal system can be confusing and intimidating for anyone not experienced with its processes and principles.

The purpose of this book is not to persuade you to hire a lawyer. That's a decision you'll have to make based on your legal needs, how much money you have, and how much you have at risk. In my experience, most judges do everything they can to accommodate people trying to represent themselves, but these non-professional are still at a huge disadvantage. Without knowledge of the law, rules, or the personalities involved, without experience in legal writing (which is confusing on purpose), public speaking or persuasion, there are lots of ways to lose your case before you feel that it has even been presented.

## 1.2    What This Book Is about and How It's Organized

When you hire a lawyer, you enter into a professional relationship usually called the attorney-client or lawyer-client relationship. In this relationship your lawyer has certain responsibilities, and you have certain expectations. You hire a lawyer to solve a problem, and you are the person who has to live with the final solution.

This book can help you:

- Understand how lawyers are made and law firms are run.
- Find the right lawyer for your problem.
- Understand the relationship between a lawyer and client.
- Get an overview of how the legal system works so you can ask good questions and understand the answers.
- Reach the best solution to your legal problem.
- Know when there has been a problem with how your lawyer has represented you and what you can do about it.

This book is organized so you can find specific information quickly. If you want to know more about how someone becomes a lawyer, go directly to Chapter 2. Turn to Chapter 13 if you believe that your lawyer has done something wrong and you want to know what to do about it.

This book has no plot, but it can be informative and useful if you decide to read it from cover to cover.

As a lawyer I was most effective in solving my client's problems when they had reasonable expectations, knew what solutions they were looking for and could understand the limitations of the legal system. A little knowledge on your part can be a huge advantage in dealing with your lawyer and ensuring that you get as much satisfaction with your result as is possible. Knowledge can also give you confidence when you must make decisions about your legal dispute.

Remember that lawyers are people too—usually intelligent and competitive people who like to win and who appreciate the income that comes with their career. It's your responsibility to be informed enough and involved enough to make decisions about where your case is going, how much is spent and what the final resolution will be.

---

**Lawyer-Client Rule Number 1**

You are hiring a lawyer to solve *your* legal problem. You have to live with the final result. Don't abandon your responsibility for the outcome to your lawyer or to the system.

---

## 1.3 How This Book Can Help You

**Confidence**. Perhaps the best way this book will help you is to give you confidence in talking to your lawyer, confidence in asking questions, and confidence in making decisions. A common characteristic between professionals and their clients is an uneven distribution of knowledge. Lawyers can be overbearing. They do things out of habit. They usually have an expectation of what the outcome of a case will be—an expectation that comes from past experience, not necessarily from your needs or desires.

I have been on both sides of the relationship: I am both a lawyer and a sophisticated buyer of legal services. I'm sure that I've occasionally been guilty of being just a little overbearing when a client has questioned my strategy; sometimes it's easier to respond with attitude than to meaningfully discuss what's happening in a case.

I've also dealt with lawyers trying to do the same with me, and it was my legal knowledge and background that helped get my lawyer's attention and handle issues in a professional way. The key to dealing with any professional is to respect the skills and abilities they've developed and still be able to acquire the knowledge necessary to meaningfully participate in the relationship.

**Reasonable Expectations**. One of my hopes is that this book will help you have reasonable expectations about the outcome of your legal problem. With some legal work, such as writing contracts or wills, you can reasonably expect a perfect product—there is no reason for a simple legal document to contain errors. But with most legal work, other parties are involved, and neither you nor your lawyer can control all of the factors of your case.

Most of my legal practice and subsequent consulting has been in the area of professional litigation, where professionals such as lawyers or doctors are sued for alleged errors by former clients. Most of these professionals believed that they had done nothing wrong and that they should win the dispute.

One of the hardest concepts for a client to understand—even a client who's a lawyer—is that nothing is guaranteed when dealing with a judge or a jury. I have never had a case where I could promise a client that we could win. A jury is only allowed to see a small part of any dispute or legal question, so any outcome is possible. As a lawyer giving advice to clients you hope to be able to determine which outcome is more probable.

No contract is so well-written that no one will ever challenge it. No will is so well-written, or the lawyer who wrote it so famous, that it can't be challenged by a family member who was "cheated." You can only hope to have good legal representation when a dispute arises.

Even with a great lawyer, the best outcome may be to find a compromise. I have advised many clients that sometimes the best thing they can do is to get the legal dispute resolved as quickly as possible and get back to living their lives.

**Strategy**. Another goal of this book is to help you assist your attorney in choosing a strategy. You should have some idea of what your strategy is before choosing your lawyer. If you suspect or believe that actually going to trial is a real possibility (less than 10% of all cases filed with courts ever go to trial), you want a lawyer who is good in trial—your personal gladiator. If you suspect that you'll try seeking a compromise, you may want to look for a different set of skills in a lawyer.

Understanding a little about the law and having a sense of what you are looking to accomplish are essential in taking responsibility for your legal problem and its solution.

**The Lawyer as a Weapon**. You'll see a number of points repeated several times in this book. One of them is that using a lawyer to punish someone won't make you happy. Some clients want to use their lawyer as big club to pound on someone. I've been approached by potential clients with an agenda that included inflicting pain on the target of their anger. I don't want the stress of representing these clients and I believe it's unethical for lawyers to become weapons.

Some lawyers, for fees paid in advance, will act as your gunfighter. Many of them will lose interest in your battle as soon as you run out of money. Then they can turn on you. Lawyers hired to punish someone are probably not looking for meaningful solutions to your problems. If you want a lawyer to destroy someone else, good luck. You'll need luck and money.

So what do you do if your opponent hires a lawyer who wants to destroy you? Find the right lawyer to represent your interests. You need someone with experience, patience, a good reputation, a good relationship with the judge and the ability to fight when fighting is required. The bad news is that lawyers with these skills and experience cost money. But they're probably cheaper than letting someone else destroy you through the legal process.

**Controlling Costs**. Which brings us to another purpose of this book—to help you control the costs of hiring a lawyer. Lawyers are expensive. Most lawyers have high expectations of their value and the compensation they should receive. Many lawyers are worth the fees they charge, but some are not. Most are honest about what and how they charge their clients and some are not.

A little knowledge about how the lawyer relationship works can go a long way in helping you take more control of the finances involved with getting your legal problem resolved. This book is like having a map of a large city in your hand when you ask your cab driver to take you somewhere you have never been—it's not a sure way to stop the driver from taking the long route but it will certainly encourage honest driving.

Another thing to remember—and many clients don't—is what the dispute is really about. It makes no sense to pay lawyers more than the value of the dispute. This is a common problem in divorce cases where clients insist on fighting over every item no matter the value. Although some items have sentimental value, you need to be aware of your motives when you are paying a lawyer $200 an hour. Be realistic about the real value of "winning."

**Being Assertive**. The last purpose of this book is to help you be more assertive. One of the biggest frustrations clients have when dealing with lawyers is feeling that they're not being listened to or taken seriously.

Most legal customers don't know what lawyers do or sell. They get impatient and frustrated. Unfortunately a lot of lawyers like it when clients are mystified by the legal process. Can you get a lawyer to patiently teach you about the law, the courts and all of your options? Yes, as long as you pay them by the hour.

Lawyers are used to making arguments. The legal process is about taking an informed position and defending it. Don't be afraid to be adamant about the results or resolution you want. But if you trust your lawyer let them do their job of finding the best way to get you there.

## 1.4  How This Book Will Probably not Help You

**Sophisticated Buyer**. This book won't transform you into a sophisticated buyer of legal services—someone who is an expert in dealing with lawyers and litigation. I have at various times been responsible for overseeing hundreds of cases in litigation at one time. My background as a lawyer definitely helped me in this role, but the biggest difference between someone like me and someone who occasionally uses a lawyer is experience.

A sophisticated buyer of legal services brings certain strengths to the table. The biggest leverage a sophisticated buyer has is the amount of work and the corresponding fees that are paid. At one point, my annual legal budget was in the tens of millions of dollars. You get a lot of customized legal services—and a lot of attention—when you have a large budget. I could dictate who worked on the file, what was done, how the status of the cases were reported and the format and timing of the bills. I asked for and received immediate attention when I needed it.

You may find yourself in a position where you have a dispute with an opponent with more resources and more experience. This doesn't mean you can't get a good result, but you must be careful in choosing your lawyer. Have reasonable expectations about the outcome. Don't give up just because your opponent is better funded.

No legal system has ever been invented that gives the average party a better chance than the American legal system. On the other hand, the one thing that will make up for a lack of experience is money. If you can spend as much as a large corporation on lawyers you probably don't need this book. Just hire a lawyer to baby-sit your other lawyers.

**Self-Representation**. The other thing that this book won't help you do is represent yourself. This is not a how-to kit. You won't find any legal forms for filing a complaint or preparing estate documents. This is about your relationship with your lawyer, not how to become one.

In addition, please read the next section very carefully.

## 1.5   The Important Legal Disclaimer

This is not a book about the law. It is a book about your relationship with your lawyer. I think I'll say this again and put it in bold print:

This is not a book about the law.

I am not making any representations regarding your specific need for a lawyer or making any promises that you will find a lawyer who will win your legal battle. No matter how good your case is you can lose—especially if you leave the final decisions to a jury.

**The law is different in every state**. The law governing most disputes between people is determined state by state. While most states follow the same basic principles, each state has differences. This is one reason lawyers tend to practice in just one state.

Many states have adopted model laws. Most of the time when I mention "the law" or "the rules," I'm referring to these model laws, the Federal Rules of Civil Procedure, or what I remember from my involvement in cases all over the country.

Be aware that the laws of one state may not apply in another state. The decisions of one state's supreme court can be ignored by all of the courts in all of the other states. A big reason to hire a local lawyer is that they know the laws where they practice.

On the other hand some cases are governed by federal law, like bankruptcy, employment cases and environmental law. Lawyers who handle these cases can often practice in many different locations, since federal law doesn't vary from state to state.

**I am not offering legal advice.** Don't sue me if your case gets messed up. **You aren't my client.** If you want some knowledge of the attorney-client relationship, our legal system, and some common sense advice on how to deal with your lawyer, read this book.

If you need legal advice, hire a lawyer.

**I will not represent you.** I am a lawyer. My background is managing complex litigation for large corporations. I am licensed to practice law in only one state, and I won't tell you which one.

You can't hire me as your lawyer; and notwithstanding my good looks and brilliance I am not who you're looking for. I don't work in private practice.

One last piece of advice. **Be aware that many legal actions have time limits** called statute of limitations. They limit how long you have to sue someone who may have wronged you. If you have been injured by someone, you may have only months or as much as a couple of years, to file a lawsuit. If a government entity is involved, you may have to provide notice within a very short period that you want to sue.

If you've been damaged because of someone else's action, please see a lawyer actively representing clients, not one writing books about hiring lawyers.

One last stylistic note—for the purpose of efficiency I'm using he, him and his pronouns when describing fictional people in this book. It is not intended to infer that all clients or lawyers are male. It's intended to be gender-neutral and makes it easier to read.

# 2. Becoming a Lawyer

*"Lawyers, I suppose, were children once."*
Charles Lamb

The Three Steps to Becoming a Lawyer:
1. A Legal Education;
2. Passing the Bar Exam, and The Character and Fitness Test; and
3. Learning to Represent Clients.

> **Lawyer-Client Rule Number 2**
> Don't be intimidated by lawyers. Knowing how lawyers are educated and licensed will help you to see them as people. Lawyers are subject to all of the same problems and motivations as the rest of us.

It's important to understand how your lawyer became a lawyer. Like most lawyers, I have several very pretty pieces of paper, mostly written in Latin, with which my clients are supposed to be appropriately impressed. These official-looking documents are important to me. They required a lot of work, they cost a lot of money and they represent an accomplishment that I am proud of. At the same time, there is nothing mysterious about what I did and you need to be less concerned about well-framed diplomas and more concerned about the quality of the lawyer's work and how well they will represent you.

There are three stages in the development of a lawyer. In law school, a lawyer learns how to understand and talk about the law. In preparing for and passing the bar examination, a lawyer learns the letter of the law. After a lawyer graduates from law school and passes the bar, he gets a job where he learns how to actually represent clients.

In order for a lawyer to represent clients, he has to be a licensed member of the state "bar" or admitted to practice law by the supreme court of the state. A state's supreme court has the responsibility of determining who can be a lawyer, making sure that lawyers remain capable and educated; and disciplining lawyers who violate the rules of conduct.

Many lawyers belong to The American Bar Association, or ABA, a voluntary organization that certifies law schools and has committees that develop model laws and recommendations on the evolution of the law. The ABA has great programs and educational sessions all over the World. (It's a lot of fun for a lawyer to go to London for a program on comparative traffic laws).

The ABA does *not* license or oversee lawyers in any state. Nor does it supervise lawyers who appear before federal judges.

## 2.1   Education

Almost every state in the country requires a potential lawyer to graduate from a law school. The exceptions are California, New York, Maine, Vermont, Virginia and Washington which each have different requirements that allow a potential lawyer to take the examination without completing law school or to substitute experience in the place of all or some of a law school education.

The other states require a potential lawyer to graduate from a law school approved by the state or the ABA. Almost all law schools require graduation from a college or university before starting law school. So for most lawyers the first step in the journey to becoming a lawyer is completing a traditional four-year program at a college or university.

There is no specific recommended program of study in college for those looking to attend law school. Many guides suggest that potential lawyers take classes or get degrees that emphasize reading comprehension and writing skills. For students who know that they want to go into a specific area of law, such as business or tax law, a degree in that area—business or accounting—makes sense. There are no specific requirements and law school provide classes in specific areas of law.

The average lawyer performed well in college, especially if they went to a prestigious law school. While the number of law school applicants varies from year to year, the general rule is that there are many more applicants than spaces for new students—sometimes hundreds of applicants for each opening.

The potential law student usually takes an exam called the Law School Admission Test™ or LSAT. Based on a combination of grades from college, scores from the LSAT, and life experiences as reflected in the application, the student is accepted to a law school and begins the educational process of becoming a lawyer.

Law schools are usually part of a larger college or university, and most major universities have a law school. A few law schools stand alone, but if they are ABA-approved they follow the same steps in providing a legal education.

Law school is different from most other programs of advanced education. Even when affiliated with a large university, the law school is a separate and distinct program, and all of the classes necessary for a law degree are taught by the law school. The exception would be if the student is seeking a dual degree, such as a law degree combined with a MBA or a master's degree in tax at the same time.

The curriculum for law school is fairly well-defined, and almost all law schools require first-year students to take the same core classes. Over the course of a three-year law-school program, more than half of the classes are required courses for all students. Many classes are graded based on performance on a single test, the final.

Law school classes are probably best known for writing assignments and the prodigious amount of reading required in each class. Most law schools use a ranking system for each graduating class, showing where the student stood in relation to the other graduates. Being at the top of his or her class can be a huge advantage for a graduating law student.

In addition to the classes required for graduation, a variety of extra-curricular activities are available to the law student. One of the most prestigious is serving as an editor of the law school's journal, or of one of the legal journals a school may publish in a specialty area.

Students can also participate in debate-type contests called moot court, where they practice courtroom and presentation skills as they compete against each other. Many law schools have a variety of opportunities for law students to represent actual clients in clinics under the supervision of licensed lawyers.

The average law program takes three years to complete, but it can be shorter or it may take longer if, for example, the student is enrolled in a dual-degree program. The student graduates after completing the program requirements. Unlike other graduate program, law school has no thesis or dissertation, although the law student spends an enormous amount of time performing research and practicing legal writing.

Just like the education at law school, the degree received is unique. The formal name of the most common legal degree is Juris Doctor or Doctor of Law (that Latin thing again), but the degree is not really a doctorate program like a medical doctor or a Ph.D., and the program is longer than a typical masters program. Law students wanting to teach law or focus on a special area of legal education can study for another year and receive a LL.M. designation or Master of Laws. The abbreviation LL.M. comes from its Latin name, Legum Magister.

Usually a law school graduate will use the initials J.D. or LL.M. to designate completion of a law school education. But for the law student, the hardest part is still to come.

## 2.2  The Bar Exam

Before a law student can practice law in most states, he must participate in a form of torture known as the bar exam. In fact, the only state that doesn't require lawyers to pass the bar exam is Wisconsin, which allows graduates of the two law schools in the state to be admitted without passing the exam. The bar exam is a test that takes two or three days to complete. It tests the prospective lawyer on the core areas of the law and on the rules of practicing law for that state. The test has several sections and is designed to be very difficult to pass.

There is a big difference between the bar exam and the material taught in law school. Law school classes focus on the development of the law and much of a student's time is spent reading, discussing, and writing about the development and history of specific areas of law.

The bar exam, on the other hand, focuses on what is called the black letter law. Black letter law is the legal standards that apply to specific legal problems today. The problem with black letter law is that it is always changing. Every time an appellate or supreme court issues a decision, the application of a law may change a little or a lot.

This is why law schools focus more on the development of the law— after all, one of the most important things that lawyers do is argue for new or different interpretations of the law for the benefit of their clients.

The bar exam poses a series of questions designed to test the student's knowledge of how the law would be applied today. To prepare for the exam, law students can take long and exhaustive courses from companies that specialize in preparing materials for big tests like the bar exam. These classes teach what the standards are when the bar exam will be taken. These classes usually last six to eight weeks, for up to twelve hours a day. They go over the laws and standards most likely to be on the bar examination. The companies that run the exam-preparation classes hire lawyers to take the exams to ensure that they know what questions are being asked.

The ability to practice law is unique to each state. Just because a lawyer is allowed to represent clients in one state does not mean that he or she can represent clients in any other state. Each state not only has a bar exam for prospective lawyers, but the exam is different for each state. They do share characteristics, and most states (all but two) use the same multiple-choice question portion, referred to as the Multi-state Bar Examination (the "MBE").

The typical bar exam has three sections: the essay portion, the MBE, and the ethics exam. The ethics exam is the easiest and can usually be taken anytime during the last year of law school, or after the formal bar exam. The ethics test is a national exam with sixty multiple-choice questions. It takes two hours. The questions are usually from the model ethical rules. A few states have written their own ethics exam and several have adapted the national exam to include local rules and special concerns of that state.

The MBE is a multiple-choice exam dealing with the main areas of the law (contracts, torts, constitutional law, criminal law, evidence, and real property). It has two hundred questions, and six hours are given to complete the exam. Even with that much time, many potential lawyers don't finish the MBE. It was developed—and is owned—by the National Conference of Bar Examiners, a non-profit organization that assists states in developing bar exams. The MBE is a difficult multiple-choice test.

When I took the MBE, for every question, only one of the answers was obviously wrong, and the other three potential answers all looked correct. It's up to the exam taker to determine which answer is the *most* correct. The questions are long and involve some of the strangest and least familiar areas of the law.

Many states grade the MBE first because it can be done by machine. In many states, if the test taker does well enough, the essay portion of the exam won't even be graded; the student will be admitted to the bar, assuming he has passed the ethics test.

The last section of the exam is the essay portion. The number of questions asked and the length of time for the test vary from state to state, but most have six to eight hours of testing with eight to twelve essay questions on all areas of law, with an emphasis on the specific law of that state. However, more states are using a standardized essay exam which is shorter and cheaper to administer for all or a part of the essay exam.

The essay portion is very intense. The answers are scored based on your ability to include as many specific points of law as you can remember. Very few people finish the entire exam. The preparation classes often suggest you write something for each question to at least get points for each one.

Because the essay test has to be graded by a person, getting the results can take a couple of months.

The bar exam is usually given twice a year. The MBE and essay portions are given in a two- or three-day period. Most states have a single location for the exam, and all recent graduates take it at the same time. I took the bar exam with almost a thousand potential lawyers crammed into a large convention room at a hotel. When I left at the end of the second day, my brain was not functioning, and I couldn't move my fingers because I had been writing for eight hours.

The bar exam is a rite of passage for graduating law students. The pressure to succeed can be immense. Law schools compare how many of their students pass on the first attempt. On average, seventy percent of bar exam participants will pass the exam. Many states allow a qualified law school graduate to take the bar exam as many times as he wants, but some states will only allow a certain number of attempts—usually three—before the student has to try a different state's bar exam, or a different career.

While passing the bar exam is a major accomplishment, it is not usually a good indication of how successful the lawyer will be. The questions test your memory and ability to regurgitate large amounts of information. The essay answers are not graded on writing ability, instead awarding points for each element of the law the test taker recognizes.

If you do find out that your lawyer had to take the bar exam a couple of times, don't be too concerned—although after three or more times, you might be concerned about how well he handles pressure. On the other hand, if your lawyer brags about his perfect score, be careful. He may have a tendency to over-prepare for everything, which is a problem when you are paying on an hourly basis.

## 2.3   Admission to Practice Law

In addition to completing law school and passing the bar exam, prospective lawyers have to apply to practice law and actually be admitted—or licensed to practice law—in the state they took the bar exam. The question is whether a potential lawyer has the "character and fitness" required to practice law. The application helps the state perform an extensive background check of the applicant to determine if there is some reason for not allowing the potential lawyer to practice law in the state.

The application is much like a job application, except the candidate has to include a lot more: education, employment history, organizations he belongs to and any problems in his past that may reflect poorly on a lawyer—up to and including parking tickets and library fines. The state's licensing organization then performs a background check that includes running a criminal history in all of the states where a candidate has lived or gone to school.

Potential lawyers can and do get turned down for admission even after completing law school and passing the bar exam and the ethics exam. While a candidate can appeal the decision, a bar organization's rejection is difficult to change, especially since it's easier to keep a potential lawyer out then it is to remove an admitted lawyer once they've been accepted. If a candidate is rejected by one state, that fact must be included in applications to any other state.

Once a candidate has graduated law school, passed the required tests and the background check, he is "admitted" to practice law in that state. He becomes a member of just that state bar, becomes subject to ethics rules and discipline by the state courts and is able to represent clients in that state.

There is no test or process that allows a lawyer to become licensed in several states at the same time. If the lawyer wants to be licensed in another state, he has to apply, and may even have to take the bar exam all over again. Some states have agreements between them that they will allow lawyers to be licensed just by completing the application without the need for taking another bar exam. These agreements are called reciprocity agreements—although they are usually between states that aren't next to each other, as states want to keep lawyers from neighboring states from coming in and competing.

Only when a lawyer has met all of these requirements is he allowed to represent clients and perform and sell legal services. If a person tries to represent someone else in a legal matter without being licensed, he can be charged with the unauthorized practice of law.

Lawyers also have to be admitted to be allowed to practice in the federal courts. Federal courts are those established under authority of the Federal Constitution, and they operate under the direction of the U. S. Supreme Court. To be admitted to practice in federal court, a lawyer usually has to be admitted to practice in a state (any state) and in good standing in that legal community. Lawyers must apply separately to every federal court district where they want to represent clients. Lawyers must apply for admission and be granted permission to appear before the supreme court of the United States.

## 2.4  Representing Clients

The day I received the letter in the mail informing me that I had passed the bar examination and had the character and fitness needed to represent clients was a great day for me and a huge source of relief for my wife. I had arrived. I was now ready to make the big bucks and tackle the hardest of legal issues, except for one small problem—I didn't have the first idea of what it meant to actually practice law!

Every year thousands of newly minted lawyers arrive to great fanfare, only to discover that the education to become real lawyers was only starting—but now, instead of paying for the education, you get paid as you learn.

Not all new lawyers join a law firm. Some never even work in a law-related profession. Government organizations, both federal and state, are huge employers of lawyers. Corporations, lobbyists, non-profits and consulting groups hire new lawyers as well. A few will start their own small law firms without any other experience, some by choice and some because jobs at law firms can be scarce. But many will start their legal careers as associates in a law firm.

The next section describes the structure of a law firm. The newest member of the firm is at the bottom of the pecking order. The new associate has great aspirations but very little knowledge of how to actually practice law. From the first day, it's like starting law school all over again. Some new associates have had experience as summer associates with a law firm. This experience is useful in understanding how a law firm operates and knowing who the members of the firm are. But life as a new associate is very different from the summer intern experience. New associates work long, boring hours; and it can be years before you work directly with clients or become a partner.

The associate lawyer has three responsibilities: learn how to practice law, learn how to develop clients, and produce revenue for the firm.

Associates do a lot of the legal research, investigation, and drafting of legal documents. They're often used for minor court appearances and for any task the partners don't want to do. This is how a new lawyer learns how to practice law. Most law firms don't have formal training for new lawyers. The partners assume, with some justification, that the new lawyers are intelligent enough to work it out on their own. Secretaries and paralegals provide a lot of the training that goes on in a law firm as new associates learn how to create legal products and navigate the legal process.

The second focus of a new associate's responsibilities, developing clients, is really something that occurs after several years. For the first year, new associates are usually not allowed any meaningful contact with clients. After that they're exposed to clients, usually with an eye towards developing credibility and building a practice of their own. One of the primary objectives of the associate is to become a partner, or owner, of the law firm. A major part of becoming partner is the ability to generate new business and create new sources of revenue.

The third responsibility of the associate is the most important: make money for the firm. In larger firms, there are more associates than partners, and the hourly billings of associates is a major source of the firm's revenue. Associates are usually paid a salary, and when they bill in excess of their salaries, the money can be distributed among the partners or used to cover the overhead of a firm. From the first day in a large firm, one of the most important measures of success for the new associate is the revenue produced billing for hourly work.

This pressure to perform and produce revenue can sometimes lead to inefficient methods of getting work done. I knew a senior associate who would handwrite all his correspondence and legal documents in longhand and then dictate the entire document into a tape recorder for transcription. His dictation had been criticized by a partner and by writing everything down he was ensuring great dictation and increased his billable hours. Not everything associates learn is for the benefit of the client.

There's a big difference in experiences between small firms and large firms. Small firms are usually less formal and hire associates because they actually have work that needs to be done. Associates in small firms are given responsibility quicker, but they're paid less than in larger firms, sometimes substantially less.

In a larger firm, associates work longer hours and are paid more money. They will usually receive more formal training and are encouraged to participate in training outside the firm. There is a more formal advancement program. An ambitious and hard-working associate has real hope of someday becoming a partner at a prestigious and successful law firm.

## 2.5 The Law Firm

The law firm is the business unit of law practice. Law firms can range in size from a single lawyer—the solo practitioner—to large, international firms consisting of thousands of lawyers and support staff. While it would seem that the mega-firms would have better lawyers and more resources, this is not the case. Most firms have good lawyers; size is not an indication of how well you'll be represented.

Most law firms, big and small, follow the same basic structure. This section briefly outlines that structure and the roles different members of the firm play.

**Partners.** Partners own the firm. A firm can have one partner or hundreds of partners who have an ownership interest. As an owner, the partner usually has some control over the management of the firm. Some firms have several kinds of "partners," so only a few lawyers actually own shares in the firm, while others share a percentage of the profits. Larger firms have managing partners and various committees headed by partners who are elected or chosen by the firm's managing partners.

Law firms are usually set up as professional corporations. Some are created when senior associates or junior partners at a large firm decide they want more control or want to focus on a different area of the law.

These lawyers then form a new firm with a new name, often using the combined last names of the founding lawyers. There is no set rule on how a law firm is named, but there are rules against misleading names and certain types of names. Using names like "Discount Legal Services & Laundry" or "Law-Mart" are discouraged. Using last names of the partners is traditional, and it also lets people know the firm's best assets—the experience and ability of the senior partners.

Sometimes a group of lawyers appear to have formed a law firm, but it might not be a firm in the traditional or legal sense. The lawyers may actually be operating their own practice or small business and sharing office space with other lawyers. In such cases, there is no central management and sometimes no relationship between the lawyers in the office. Sometimes you can tell when lawyers are sharing an office because every lawyer is identified as a separate professional corporation. Other times it's not so clear, when the office has a name that looks like a law firm.

One of the things you need to understand before hiring a lawyer is how a particular law firm is structured and what the relationship is between lawyers in the same office.

**Associates.** Lawyers who don't own part of the business are usually called *associates.* The new lawyer hired into the firm is an associate. So is the lawyer who's been with a firm for ten years but doesn't own a portion of it. Firms may distinguish between junior and senior associates, usually to let clients know if a lawyer has more experience or bills more per hour.

Most firms have a partnership track. When an associate joins the firm, there's an expectation that after a certain number of years the associate will become eligible to be considered or voted on to become a partner. The average partnership track is seven years, although it can be as many as ten and as few as four or five. Criteria for becoming a partner is different at each firm but usually depends on the lawyer's value to the firm in terms of legal ability, clients, or revenue brought in.

When an associate becomes eligible for partnership, the other partners vote on whether to make the associate a partner or wait another year. In large firms, there may be more associates eligible than there are openings, so only the shining stars make it. New partners usually have to pay for their new ownership interest but are able to participate in management activities and share in the firm's profits.

**Of Counsel.** Sometimes an experienced lawyer may decide to work with a firm without being a partner or even handling the same type of work the firm handles. A lawyer who is part of the office but not really part of the firm is referred to as *of counsel*. A lawyer who is of counsel may be included in the letterhead and may be allowed to participate in the management of the firm but usually the relationship is more akin to a solo-practitioner renting an office and sharing resources.

**Employees.** Law firms also hire non-lawyer employees who support the business and the lawyers. These include paralegals who are licensed to provide limited legal services, secretaries, clerks, and others who provide special services. Some firms hire nurses to review medical records; patent law firms often use engineers to review complex documents. While many of these services can be provided by outside consultants, larger firms often save money and get more consistent results by hiring full-time employees with these skills.

**Solo-Practitioner.** The solo-practitioner is a lawyer who practices law alone. He may have a secretary or paralegal to help, but there are no other lawyers helping him represent clients. Many excellent lawyers are solo-practitioners, some because they enjoy the flexibility of being on their own, and others because they dislike law firm politics. A big advantage for a client using a solo-practitioner can be finding a great lawyer at a reasonable price. A downside can be the lack of resources and backup if something happens to your lawyer.

There are as many different kinds of law firms as there are restaurants. See Chapter 4 for examples. The key is for you to find not only the right lawyer, but to understand the resources of the firm and how it is structured.

## 2.6   Continuing Legal Education and Accomplishments

Almost all states require lawyers to take classes on a regular basis to help them stay current on changes in the law. Lawyers can choose from a wide variety of topics, as long as they take some courses on ethics. These classes are usually taught by other lawyers and are provided by the state bar organization or private companies.

Lawyers also will often join associations that focus on their specific area of law. Organizations exist for most law specialties at both the state and national level. They also offer courses and networking, and they often publish legal journals on their specialty.

If a lawyer includes his membership in a specific organization in his bio, it may sound impressive, but generally the only significance is that the lawyer has focused his practice in a specific area.

Lawyers also distinguish themselves based on serving in local or national legal organizations or publishing articles on a specialized topic. All of these activities demonstrate the focus of a lawyer's practice.

# 3. Types of Law and Expertise

*"I don't want to know what the law is;
I want to know who the judge is."*
*Roy Cohn*

## 3.1 A Very Short History of the Law

Most law in our country was developed from the English legal system that had developed for over five hundred years before the birth of the United States. The structure we inherited and still use today is based on the two different sources of law that developed there: statutory law and common law.

**Statutory Law** is law created by a legislative body. In the United States, federal or state legislatures pass laws which are signed into law by the president or governor. These laws are then interpreted and enforced by the courts. Most people are familiar with the process of how a bill is proposed in Congress and then passed as a law or statute. Once a statute has been passed, it is the law of the land until a subsequent statute is passed that changes the law.

**Common Law** is law created by a judge to resolve a specific problem. The judge's decision acts as a guide when a similar problem comes up again. Long before the English parliament started passing laws, decisions were made by common, or court-made, law.

Starting in the twelfth century, English monarchs and local authorities recognized the need for consistency in how decisions were made and the law was applied. For example, the courts created the rules about how contracts are made or when the sale of property takes place. These rules—or decisions made by judges—were called precedent, and only when there were new situations was there need for new law to be created.

Many standards we use today come from these previous court decisions, although some have since been made more official by a state or federal legislature passing a law covering the same area. For example, it was common—or judge-created—law that first defined the requirements of a binding and enforceable contract. Since then, legislatures have passed laws on different kinds of contracts, and when and how they are to be enforced. But they follow the same basic principles and use the same four requirements that the English courts developed over 500 years ago.

When a common law rule and a statutory law clash with each other, the statutory law usually wins. This is based on the English solution for occasions when the common law conflicted with what the King wanted—the King always won.

**Remedies: Equity and Legal**. Another distinction developed by the English was the difference between equitable and legal remedies. In the English courts, judges could award damages or money to the winner. This was a legal remedy.

But sometimes money wasn't enough to help a plaintiff, so the winner would appeal to the King for equity, or a remedy that wasn't money but forced someone to do something. For example, if someone stole your home, you might not want money; you want your home back. If all you could recover was money, someone could force you to sell your home by moving in while you were gone. The equitable solution was to have your property returned to you, but only the King had the power to give your home back to you, which was an equitable decision.

REMEDY: When you sue or when you are sued, the party filing the litigation seeks a specific solution, called the remedy. In some cases, the plaintiff asks for money—a legal remedy. In other cases, the plaintiff wants a contract to be enforced and that the other person be forced to give the thing or property claimed as theirs—an equitable remedy.

For a long time in England, legal remedies and equitable remedies were given in different courts and had different kinds of trial. Historically, an equitable remedy could be awarded only by a judge; there was no right to a jury trial.

Early in our country's history, you could ask for only one type of remedy. If you wanted both, you had to sue twice in two different courts. Only Delaware still has separate courts for these separate kinds of relief, although in a few other states, different judges in the same district will decide the legal and equitable issues of the same case. This can create problems when suing for both legal and equitable remedies—for example, if you not only want your home back, but also money for damages to it.

## 3.2   Types of Law

As a result of the increasing complexity of our society and laws, many different areas of law have developed, with more every year. As the law becomes more complex, lawyers require more time and expertise to be able to represent clients.

The major division of law is the most simple: criminal and civil. In many areas, criminal and civil cases are handled in different courts. Many criminal defense lawyers practice only criminal law.

**Criminal Law** involves cases where a person has been accused of committing a crime. The first key element of a criminal case is that the defendant is an individual or corporation accused of having violated a criminal statute. There are no common-law—court-created—criminal laws, only those passed by a state legislature or by the federal government.

The second key element of a criminal case is that the purpose of the action is to punish the wrongdoer. It usually involves the freedom of the defendant. The prosecutor works for the government, and, unlike other areas of law, the defendant is entitled to be represented by a lawyer. If a defendant in a criminal case cannot afford a lawyer, the governmental entity bringing the charges must provide one. These lawyers are usually from an agency or office of public defenders, although the court may appoint a member of the local bar to represent a defendant. In really big cases, a prominent or ambitious lawyer may volunteer for the notoriety a publicized case can bring.

Here are some of the specialties that exist within criminal law:

| | | |
|---|---|---|
| FELONY | DRUG CRIMES | TRAFFIC VIOLATIONS |
| MISDEMEANOR | DUI/DWI | CRIMINAL APPEALS |
| DOMESTIC VIOLENCE | JUVENILE CRIMES | |
| WHITE-COLLAR CRIMES | PAROLE/PROBATION | |

Many lawyers who focus on defending clients in criminal cases started as prosecutors or public defenders. Expertise is developed by prosecuting cases. Success is usually measured by winning big cases. However, the ability to work with the judge and the prosecutors is often as important as expertise when helping clients facing criminal penalties.

**Civil Law** is pretty much everything else. While most civil cases involve two people or organizations suing each other, even a government entity can be a party in a civil case. Most of us are familiar with areas of civil law like divorce law, injury law and bankruptcy law, but look at the list of specialties to see how many different areas of law there are:

| | | |
|---|---|---|
| APPEALS | ELDER LAW | MERGERS & ACQUISITIONS |
| ADMIRALTY LAW | EMINENT DOMAIN | MILITARY LAW |
| AVIATION LAW | EMPLOYEE BENEFITS | PERSONAL INJURY |
| BANKING LAW | ENTERTAINMENT LAW | PRODUCTS LIABILITY |
| BANKRUPTCY | ENVIRONMENTAL LAW | REAL ESTATE |
| BUSINESS LAW | FAMILY LAW | SECURITIES |
| CHARITIES | FINANCE | SOCIAL SECURITY |
| CIVIL RIGHTS | HEALTH CARE | TAX LAW |
| CLASS ACTIONS | IMMIGRATION LAW | TOXIC TORTS |
| COMMUNICATIONS & MEDIA LAW | INSURANCE LAW | TRUSTS AND ESTATES |
| CONSTRUCTION LAW | INTELLECTUAL PROPERTY | WHITE COLLAR CRIME |
| CONSUMER LAW | INTERNATIONAL LAW | WILLS AND PROBATE |
| CONTRACTS | INTERNET LAW | WORKER'S COMP |
| DEBTOR AND CREDITOR | LABOR & EMPLOYMENT | ZONING & LAND USE |
| EDUCATION LAW | LEGAL MALPRACTICE | |
| | MEDICAL MALPRACTICE | |

Most lawyers develop expertise in several related areas, such as injury law and insurance law. Some lawyers and even some law firms specialize in representing a specific kind of client, such as businesses, but will handle all kinds of law for their business clients.

The most important thing is to realize that not all lawyers have experience in handling all kinds of cases. The best way to know if yours has the experience you need is to ask what kind of case yours is and how many cases of that type a lawyer has handled.

A good lawyer will be honest with you and busy enough that he won't want to take a case that is outside his expertise. The last thing you want is to have problems develop because the lawyer you used for your divorce tries to handle an injury case and makes a mistake.

### 3.3 How Lawyers Specialize

It's important to understand that some "specialties" are more marketing strategy than real expertise. Ask questions and take the time to do research. Remember that lawyers are trained to talk, so don't rely just on what they say when trying to decide if a lawyer has the skill or experience you need.

A lawyer can specialize in a number of ways. None of them alone will ensure that a lawyer really has the expertise you want.

**Education.** The first way to determine if a lawyer has expertise in a specific area is to look at their education and work experience. While very few law schools specialize in just one area of the law, some do have reputations for special programs.

When you interview several lawyers, you may realize that they share common work and professional experience. For example, lawyers who specialize in tax law will often have an accounting background and may have worked for the IRS for several years to prepare them for private practice. Many lawyers who practice patent law will have a background in a technical field.

Another aspect of education is participation in a program or certification from an organization for a specialty. If your lawyer says he has completed a special program, find out what the program required. Some programs can take years to finish, while others hand out a certificate after a weekend seminar in an exotic location. Be impressed, but also be aware.

**Experience.** Probably the most common way for a lawyer to develop expertise is by practicing that type of law. Find out what percentage of a lawyer's practice is made up of cases like yours. Ask about previous cases that are similar. For formal litigation in a court, ask about specific cases to see if your lawyer has handled any high-profile cases or appeals that resulted in a written opinion. While the opinion may not mean much to you, you may be able to get a sense of that type of case and gain some insight on the level of expertise a lawyer has developed.

**Court Admission.** In some areas of law, a lawyer has to be admitted to a special court in order to practice. This is true of patent law, bankruptcy and maritime law. A lawyer also has to be admitted to practice in federal courts. Make sure that your prospective lawyer has already been admitted to the court where your matter will be handled.

**Teaching and Articles.** Another way to get a sense of a lawyer's expertise is if the lawyer teaches at a law school or has taught special classes for other lawyers for maintaining their licenses.

Ask if your lawyer has ever presented or taught that kind of class. If he has, and ask for a course syllabus or brochure that may describe the lawyer's background and experience in that area of the law.

Some lawyers write articles for local legal magazines or newspapers. These articles are usually a good indication that the lawyer has some expertise and is known for that expertise in the local legal community.

**Membership.** Many lawyers belong to, and are involved in, organizations within their specialty. Lawyers write articles for journals published by these organizations, give presentations, and may serve in local or national leadership positions. All of these activities help a lawyer stay current and network with other professionals who practice the same kind of law.

## 3.4  Measuring Expertise

Expertise can be very hard to measure. And how much expertise your matter requires is something you'll have to determine. A lawyer with lots of experience and a huge reputation—but who won't listen to you or pay attention to your case—is probably not what you want.

A lawyer with a great reputation and the most experience may charge more for his time than you'll really need or want to pay. On the other hand, a new lawyer looking to develop expertise and make his reputation may be exactly what you're looking for, depending on the nature of your problem and what's at stake.

The next chapter discusses some of the factors you need to consider before hiring a lawyer. Expertise is important and the right expertise may be worth spending more money for. When evaluating expertise consider all of the lawyer's activities and previous experiences.

# 4. How to Find Your Lawyer

*"A jury consists of twelve persons chosen to decide
who has the better lawyer."*
Robert Frost

Choosing your lawyer is a very important, and potentially daunting, task. Most people want to hire a lawyer who looks and sounds like a Hollywood star for as little money as possible. While finding a lawyer who can talk well is not usually a problem, your job is to be as educated as possible about who your lawyer is, what he is good at, and what it will cost you.

You need to understand exactly who will be working on your file and what resources a firm has to offer. Whether you are paying a little or a lot for your legal representation, ask questions about why and what you are getting for your money. When a lawyer tells you about his resources or ability, or he promises an outcome in your dispute, get it in writing.

## 4.1 Law Firms

The law firm is a business offering legal products to you as a consumer. A law firm can be one person or thousands of lawyers and employees who support the business of practicing law.

See Chapter 2 for more information on how law firms are organized and managed. A law firm is a business, and as such, they're always looking for customers who will buy their services and products.

This section outlines and briefly describes a few of the different kinds of businesses that exist to sell legal services.

**Solo Firms** are easy to describe: they consist of one lawyer selling his services and representing clients. Many good lawyers practice in solo law firms, sometimes with a staff and sometimes alone. Technology has made it easy to do many of the tasks that once required a trained legal secretary, but many solo lawyers like having support and use paralegals and other staff to help increase the number of clients they can help.

Many solo law firms share office space with other lawyers or with larger firms. This allows them to have access to support and resources without the expense of running their own office. Make sure you understand whether your lawyer works alone or is part of a larger firm. Know what resources your lawyer has to handle your representation.

One of the potential downsides of hiring a solo law firm is that there are no other lawyers to turn to if something happens to your lawyer. Make sure there's a backup plan in place and find out if there's an agreement with another lawyer to help out if needed. Some lawyers have agreements with colleagues to cover cases for them when they have a conflict or an emergency. If this is the case, take time to meet the backup lawyer and make sure you have confidence in him.

Some of the best lawyers I've met work as solo practitioners. For many clients this can be the best combination of finding someone experienced and controlling costs.

When thinking about hiring a solo practitioner, avoid lawyers who:

1) Move offices often. A good sign for clients is a stable, solo law firm that's been in the same location for a while. If the lawyer has just opened his law firm or moved recently, look for signs of permanency, such as a comfortable environment, other lawyers who have been in the office for some time, and an effort to decorate or develop a professional-looking office.
2) Make lots of promises but won't put anything in writing. See Chapter 11 for descriptions of the documentation you should be receiving.
3) Are unorganized or unable to recall the facts of your case. There's no excuse today for a lawyer who doesn't use computer software to keep track of clients, deadlines and documents. If it becomes clear that the lawyer isn't keeping up, take some initiative and request appropriate attention for your problem or find another lawyer.
4) Appear to be too busy. If you have trouble getting a hold of your lawyer, he may have too many clients. A common characteristic of successful lawyers is an inability to refuse a new case when they are really too busy. The advantage a larger firm has is that they have other lawyers available to do your work. On the other hand, with a large firm the lawyer you hired may never actually work on your file.

**General Practice Law Firms** are formed with several lawyers and offer a variety of legal services. Usually in a general practice law firm, the founding partners each have a different expertise. They hope that by forming a firm, they'll be able to attract more clients and provide more legal services.

The advantage for you is that this kind of firm has resources and expertise in a wide variety of legal specialties. There may be a lawyer to prepare your will and another to handle traffic tickets. In addition, a good general practice law firm will have the resources to handle more complicated cases.

The focus of a general law firm is wide spectrum of legal services, not to support or market one specific specialty. If you're looking for good quality legal work at a reasonable price, a local general practice law firm may be one of your best options.

**Boutique Firms** are usually identified by their smaller size and focus on one specific area of law. A boutique firm is usually started when a group of lawyers who all practice the same kind of law form a law firm. These lawyers may know each other in the legal community and may even be from a bigger law firm and decide to go off on their own. An advantage for the boutique firm is being able to focus on one type of law and market that specialty.

The boutique firm can be more selective in what work they take and with which clients they represent, whereas a specialist in a general practice law firm may not be able to refuse work from a client. Boutique firms usually hold themselves out as experts in one area of law and most of the lawyers in the firm practice that kind of law.

Examples of boutique firms include tax law, criminal defense, business transaction and personal injury law firms. Because these firms focus on just one area of the law, they generally have more resources and more collective experience. If you have a complicated legal issue in a specialized area, you'll probably want to talk to a lawyer at a boutique firm with that focus.

Lawyers in a boutique law firm are more expensive on an hourly basis than other kinds of firms because they hold themselves out as experts and because of efficiency in handling cases. While their hourly rates can be higher, their expertise can make them more cost-effective overall.

**Silk Stocking Firms** are usually larger. They're easy to spot; no cost is spared to impress the client and provide a comfortable environment for the lawyers. The lobby is large, and there is liberal use of expensive wood and marble throughout.

The silk stocking firm usually has a long history or prestigious story about how it was started. Silk stocking law firms earned this name because of the expensive and fashionable dress requirements of attorneys who practice there. They usually hire only the top students from the top law schools. They have enormous resources and support staff and market their services as a top law firm in the community. Many of the partners are involved in civic and non-profit organizations.

Silk stocking law firms can also be boutique firms, specializing in only a few areas of law practice, but many of them are general practice firms and have several departments, each organized like a boutique firm so that the firm can provide a wide range of legal services to their clients. The work they provide is usually very high quality, and the lawyers who make partner are generally excellent lawyers.

The biggest downside of a silk stocking law firm is that every decoration for the office and every car provided for the partners is paid for by the clients. A silk stocking law firm is about money. Many market themselves as expensive, and thus exclusive. They charge high rates and involve large groups of lawyers on every case to assure that nothing is missed.

If money is no object, and you want to ensure a reasonably good outcome, then consider meeting with lawyers from a silk stocking law firm.

**International Firms** are the largest of the large. These firms don't just practice international law; instead, they're international in the sense that they have offices all over the world. This kind of firm is often also a silk stocking law firm.

Only the best lawyers from the best schools practice here, and the rates reflect that. The biggest difference between the local big firm and the international firm is that the latter has offices in every large city in the United States and in several foreign countries.

Clients need this kind of expertise when there's a legal problem or issue in several countries. Large, multi-national businesses hire these firms for their ability to handle legal issues all over the world and for the reputation and ability of specific lawyers in local offices.

**Legal Stores** are a fairly new kind of law office. They usually have a name telling you what kind of legal product or service they sell, such as, "Family Law Office" or "Wills and Trusts Law Office."

The business model for a legal store is often more like Wal-Mart than the traditional law firm. They've developed a process for handling just one kind of law and they try to do it at the cheapest possible cost for the client. This type of firm can be a good option if you need a simple will or have a typical legal dispute that fits in their model.

Avoid using a legal store for complex legal issues. Don't use the "Wills and Trusts Law Firm" for your estate planning if you have a complicated estate or large business that you want to transfer to your children. Don't expect to have much contact with a partner or even with a lawyer. Many legal stores use paralegals and assistants to meet with clients and do most of the legal work.

**Client Mills** are less a specific firm type and are more of a philosophy followed by law firms in all of these firm types. The principle attribute of the client mill is a single focus on making money for the lawyers.

The best way to recognize a client mill is when a lawyer appears to be willing to say anything to get your legal work, wants significant money in advance of doing any work, or when a legal matter goes on without any possible resolution.

Personal injury firms are client mills if they sign up clients and look for easy settlements without doing real work or investigation. Avoid any firm that wants an excessive amount of money before doing any work or appears to be neglecting your legal case once they've signed you up.

If you never meet the lawyer—and meet with paralegals or assistants instead—be concerned. Likewise, if the lobby looks more like a waiting room than a lobby, be aware that the firm may be taking on too many clients and that none of them are getting great legal services.

## 4.2  What You Should Be Looking for

The lawyer you should be looking for depends on a number of factors: the nature of the legal dispute or the services you need; where the dispute needs to be resolved; and, most importantly, how much you're at risk to lose.

Not every case or problem requires or justifies the very best lawyer. In some cases, it makes sense to hire a younger, hungrier lawyer with limited experience but with the desire and time to help you.

With an older and more experienced lawyer you gain experience with the law, judges and other lawyers. With luck, the higher hourly fee will be offset by the fact that it takes less time to do the same work and perhaps get a better result.

What you are trying to avoid is the young lawyer who charges too large a fee because of ego (or greed), or the experienced lawyer who takes too much time to get your work done because of caution (or greed).

There is no fail-proof system for finding just the right lawyer. Make sure you like your lawyer and that he communicates with you on a regular basis. Here are some factors you can explore when interviewing lawyers and deciding who you want to hire.

**Education.** Make sure that your lawyer actually attended an approved law school, graduated, passed the state bar exam, and was admitted to practice law. After that, it's not clear that education has any impact of the quality of the legal services you'll receive. The best lawyers don't always go to the best law schools. Most law schools are good. The criteria for getting into any law school require all lawyers to be reasonably intelligent.

What may be more important than law school is the other education your lawyer has had. For example, tax lawyers usually have an accounting education and many have earned a CPA. This type of non-legal education can be very important in finding a good lawyer, so ask about their under-graduate studies and educational background.

**Experience.** How much experience does your lawyer have? Experience is the best teacher of the law. Find out about other clients with legal problems like yours. Ask about other similar cases, trial experiences, and trial results. Ask about your lawyer's appellate cases. Ask other lawyers about your lawyer's reputation and their experiences with him.

**Reputation.** It's hard to evaluate a lawyer's reputation, but a couple of resources can help. The first is a national directory of lawyers provided by Martindale-Hubbell (www.martindale.com). Lawyers have to pay to be included the directory and the lawyer or firm supplies most of the information. The profiles on individual lawyers may provide their background and an overview of his participation in the community.

Martindale-Hubbell sends out surveys asking lawyers to rate other lawyers in their same field, and the directory uses a resulting rating system. The ratings are a good tool for getting a general sense what other lawyers think about a specific lawyer. The best rating is AV for superior lawyers who've practiced for more than ten years. If your lawyer is listed in Martindale-Hubbell but has no rating, ask why.

A second way to get an opinion of a lawyer's reputation is to ask another lawyer. See Section 4.3 for the best way to get a lawyer's candid opinion.

**Communication.** One vital aspect of your relationship with your lawyer will be the ability to communicate well with each other. You can do several things in the first interview to determine whether communication between you is going to be an issue.

Ask questions and take notes. Don't be concerned about asking "dumb" questions. How patient is your lawyer in answering basic questions or questions about his qualifications? Remember to listen to the answer when you ask something. Take notes to keep track of both the lawyer's responses and your impressions of them.

**Law Firm.** Remember that everyone in the law firm you're retaining will have access to your personal documents. Much of the work will be done by the associates, paralegals and secretaries as part of your legal team. Make sure you're comfortable with all of these people. Get a sense of how the members of the firm interact. If you can, find out how long the staff and members of a firm have been together. One indication of a firm with problems is a high turnover of employees.

---

### Lawyer-Client Rule Number 3

Ask "dumb" questions in a smart way. Be prepared with questions you want to ask. Document the answers. Respect the lawyer's time, but don't be afraid to ask a question.

---

## 4.3  Identifying the Expertise You Need

The best way to get the information to make an informed decision on which lawyer to hire is to ask lots of questions. I was always amazed when meeting with clients for the first time by how few questions they asked. If I looked like and talked like a lawyer, it was good enough for most of them. Many clients are perfectly content with the first lawyer they stumble on until something goes wrong or they begin to realize they aren't getting the outcome they hoped for.

The questions you ask should help you evaluate the lawyer's level of expertise, your comfort level with the lawyer, and how well he explains what you need to know. Don't ever let a professional get away with not answering your questions because the answer would be "too complicated." This is *your* legal problem, and one of your obligations is to understand the big issues. A lawyer who lacks the ability or patience to answer your questions in an interview will probably not become more responsive later on.

**The Firm's Website.** Start your research here. Read the biographies of the lawyers you'll be meeting as well as those of the other partners in the firm. Keep in mind that websites are marketing tools and might overstate a lawyer's abilities. Look at how the law firm represents itself and what the lawyers claim to be good at. Check the organizations the lawyer belongs to and what other activities the lawyer gives detail on. After visiting the firm's website, look at other resources online like Martindale Hubbell (www.martindale.com) and Find Law (www.findlaw.com). See how the lawyer is rated and review their biographical information.

Lawyers building a reputation in a specialty will often write in that area of law, so another great way to get more information is by looking at the articles, books, or chapters for books they've written. If the lawyer's bio provides titles of written materials, try to get copies of items that seem related to your legal issue. Don't be impressed just because your lawyer has written articles; make sure they're related to the kind of expertise you need.

**Affiliations.** Find out if your lawyer belongs to organizations related to your legal problem. If they're involved in a local or national organization, they'll be happy to tell you about not only their participation, but also if they've been a leader in it. Find out if they have taught any classes for other lawyers or at a school. And see if they have any professional designations or further education in their specialty.

**Interviews.** Use the interviews you have with prospective lawyers to ask what kind of expertise they think is required for your type of case;

what does the lawyer think you should be looking for? If you're looking for a lawyer to handle your divorce, tell the lawyer about facts or circumstances that might make it an unusual case, such as property in another state or country, assets that came from one side of the family or the other, or special circumstances about children. Make sure the lawyer can easily explain whether these elements are important and how he'll work with you.

Remember that no lawyer has ever handled your case before so no one can anticipate every issue that'll come up. What a lawyer answers may not be as important as *how* he answers. Most lawyers will need to do research for every case to see how the law applies to its unique facts.

A less-experienced lawyer will have to do more research, but should charge less for his time. A more experienced lawyer will do less research but will charge more for that experience. What you want to avoid is the expensive lawyer who still does a lot of research.

In the end, experience may not be what's most important. You might be more concerned about whether you can communicate with your lawyer and whether you feel confident that he'll do everything he can to get you the best outcome. Sometimes the best lawyer is the one who not only believes in you and your side, but will tell you if you're not going to win.

---

**Lawyer-Client Rule Number 4**

Take the time to find the best lawyer for you. Research, get recommendations and interview several lawyers. Don't hire the first lawyer you talk to unless time is limited and who you hire will have little impact on the outcome.

---

## 4.4  How to Find a Lawyer

Hopefully, by now you have a little better idea of what you're looking for in a lawyer and have some ideas about questions you can ask. But how do you actually find a lawyer when you need one?

**Recommendations.** One of the most common ways to find a lawyer is through the recommendation from a friend, co-worker or family member. If you plan to hire a lawyer based on a recommendation, think about how well your source really knows the lawyer and whether the person giving the recommendation is qualified to give an informed opinion. Your friend or co-worker may not have asked the right questions or even know if they got the best result. When getting recommendations, consider how much weight you should give them and how much experience and knowledge your recommenders have.

**Directory.** If you still have yellow pages, the lawyers section is the largest one. Most directory listings provide very little information other than the area of law the firm practices in and perhaps some marketing information.

**Internet.** Numerous online services and directories can help you find a lawyer. Most are independent, but some directories are owned by specific law firms and use them to point clients toward them.

Internet services usually provide more information about law firms than a phone book, but the information is not necessarily more reliable. These services may also provide links to a law firm's website, and sometimes they provide reviews by clients. Most internet directories charge law firms to be included and simply post the information provided by the firms.

One internet resource available in most states is a directory maintained by the state bar association. Some states even have a referral program that will recommend a lawyer in a specialty. These services are not based on any specific expertise, and as long as a lawyer is in good standing with the state bar he's included in the directory and can participate in the referral program.

**Pay a Lawyer to Find a Lawyer.** Find a lawyer in the area of law you need and call for an appointment. Or find a website for a local legal organization, like a chapter of the state bar organization in the area of law you need, and contact the current president of that organization. Explain that you need help finding a lawyer and that you're willing to pay for the lawyer's time to get three recommendations.

When making the appointment, be clear about what help you're looking for; don't play games or make the lawyer think that he's getting a new client. Be willing to pay a reasonable fee for his help. Promise to keep his recommendations confidential. *Make sure that the lawyer you're paying for advice isn't receiving any other compensation for making recommendations.* You're paying for legal advice, so be clear what you want and the type of lawyer you are looking for.

Sometimes the best resource is a lawyer on the other side of your type of dispute. If you want a good personal injury lawyer for example, you might want to ask a personal injury *defense* lawyer—who usually works for insurance companies—to make a recommendation of lawyers you should talk to.

Not all lawyers will agree to help you. Some will want to represent you themselves and won't be willing to make recommendations. Others don't want to get involved in making value judgments about their peers. But with a little research and a few phone calls, you should be able to get some guidance and be able to identify several candidates. This may cost a little money, but remember you're going to spend thousands of dollars. Isn't it worth a little money and time in the beginning of the case to find the right lawyer instead of taking a risk on someone you don't know?

**Interview Several Potential Lawyers.** Unless the outcome isn't very important and it's clear that everyone charges about the same, take the time to interview several lawyers.

If you're looking for help handling a speeding ticket, who you hire may not matter so much if they've handled tickets. Interviewing three lawyers might be overkill. But if your freedom, your livelihood, or your life savings is at stake, take responsibility for finding the right lawyer.

Interviewing multiple lawyers gives you several significant advantages. The first and most obvious is having several to compare and choose from. The second is that you can learn a lot about your case as you ask questions and meet lawyers. The last advantage is that you will become a more sophisticated client as you conduct interviews and better able to make decisions.

Lawyers can be concerned about conflicts of interest because of an interview (see Section 12.2). Once a lawyer has talked to you, he cannot ethically represent the other side of the conflict. This can be an issue in a smaller town where only a few lawyers are involved in most of the cases.

If a lawyer asks you if you are interviewing other lawyers, be truthful but firm in your desire to meet others. To avoid conflicts, lawyers sometime charge for an initial interview. In personal injury cases, lawyers rarely charge for an initial interview and conflicts are rare, because lawyers who represent injured plaintiffs don't usually represent defendants in the same kinds of cases. Don't be talked out of interviewing other lawyers by someone who wants your money.

**Appointed Lawyers.** A unique relationship exists when a lawyer is hired *for* you. Two instances are most common. The first is when an insurance company hires a lawyer for you when you are sued and the allegations are covered by insurance. This lawyer is usually called an insurance defense lawyer.

The second instance is when you're a defendant in a criminal case and the court appoints a defense lawyer; either a local lawyer or from the public defender's office.

In the insurance company situation, you have little choice when your insurer hires your lawyer, and most of the time that isn't a problem. Because the insurance company pays damages, they have an incentive to hire someone experienced who can defend you well.

In some circumstances, where all of the damages aren't covered by your insurance, you need to be concerned about the quality of the lawyer hired for you. You may even want to hire your own lawyer to watch the case and advise you on how to get the best outcome.

Sometimes, even if insurance covers all of the potential damages, you may still not get along with your appointed lawyer. Discuss your concerns with your insurance company, and if necessary ask for another lawyer.

In the second situation, if you are a criminal defendant you probably have the right to ask for another lawyer. Just remember that the situation may not get any better with a different lawyer. Criminal defendants receive public defenders because they can't afford counsel. Public defenders and those appointed to provide a defense are often underappreciated and overly busy.

## 4.5   The Interview: What to Ask

Considering all the potential questions you could ask, you might think that interviewing a lawyer will be an all-day task. That's not true. While it's important to get the information you need to make a decision, it's also important to realize that the lawyer's time is valuable.

Your initial interview should have two different goals: 1) tell the lawyer what he needs to know about your legal issue, and 2) get enough information to make a decision on whether to hire the lawyer.

The first part of the process should be led by the lawyer. The second part is your responsibility and can usually be completed in less than 30 minutes. Let the lawyer go first so he knows what he needs to about you and your specific legal issue. Many lawyers will spend a lot of the interview talking about themselves and their experience. You may find that the lawyer answers many of your questions before you ask them, so the rest of the interview may just be a matter of filling in the blanks.

Some firms will ask you to fill out a questionnaire or survey before you meet with a lawyer. Make sure you keep a copy of the completed survey and take it to the interview with you. Sometimes a paralegal will perform the first interview. Make sure you have the chance to conduct your own interview with the lawyer who is handling your case before you make a hiring decision. Here are some general categories of questions you can ask.

**Interest.** Start by confirming that the lawyer is interested in and has the time to take represent you. If the lawyer doesn't want the case or if he's not the right lawyer for that type of problem, find out as soon as possible. Don't be offended if the lawyer isn't interested; be glad that he's being candid with you. If the lawyer doesn't want the case or can't take it because of a conflict, ask for a recommendation of other lawyers to talk to.

**Expertise.** Ask the lawyer what he's an expert in and how did he develop his expertise? If a lawyer's marketing material indicates that he handles a different kind of law, make sure you get information about his experience handling your kind of legal issue. For example, if a friend refers you to a divorce lawyer for your personal injury case, the lawyer may be interested in your case but you need to make sure that both the lawyer and the firm have the ability to handle it.

**Similar Cases.** In confirming expertise ask specifically about similar cases the lawyer has handled and the best results that he has gotten for other clients. Be aware that good results in other cases don't necessarily indicate what will happen in yours. Lawyers love to tell war stories, so ask for a couple that are similar to your situation.

**Initial Thoughts.** Ask the lawyer for his initial impression about your issue. What are his concerns? What he will need to evaluate or investigate? What issues might come up as the case develops? What does he know about lawyers who might represent the other side of the dispute? If a lawsuit has already been filed, ask the lawyer about the judge and his experience in that court. Try to get a sense of his thoughts or whether the lawyer is really even thinking about it yet.

**Specific Case Questions.** You may have specific questions about the facts or issues related to your problem or questions that came to you when the lawyer asked his initial interview questions. Write these questions down so you don't forget to ask them.

**Meet the Team.** Ask the lawyer to identify all of the members of the firm who will work on your file. At some point before hiring a lawyer you should meet all of the members of the firm who will have access to your personal information and who will be working on documents or evaluating the case. Try to get an idea of how legal work is handled in the firm. It's not a bad thing for most of the work to be done by an experienced associate; just make sure you know it when you hire the firm.

In some situations, you may want to have a second interview with a junior partner or associate if they will be handling most of the actual work on your file.

**Billing.** Ask straightforward questions about the cost of the services you are purchasing. If work is done on an hourly basis, ask for a written summary of how costs and fees are billed, the hourly rate for everyone who will work on the file, and an estimate of the total cost of the case to the anticipated conclusion.

Discuss how often bills will be received and how much detail will be provided. If the fee is a set fee or contingency fee, you need to determine how costs will be handled and whether you will receive regular summaries of costs as they are incurred. Costs and fees are not the same thing. Fees are the cost of the lawyer's time, costs are the expenses of the legal process such as filing, mailing or expert costs.

**Time Frame.** Find out what a normal timeframe would be for this type of legal case. What are the major events, and when would they occur? How long should it take to get matter resolved—understanding that there are often unforeseen delays?

**Plan of Action.** Ask what actions the lawyer would take first to investigate and evaluate your problem if you hire him. What would be his plan of action?

**History and Background.** Where has the lawyer practiced law, and how long he has been with his current firm? If he has a web site and it includes a biography, let the lawyer know that you've read it. Ask if it is up to date or if other, more recent, professional experiences are missing. Ask if he had any professional or work experience prior to practicing law that relate to handling your case. If the lawyer is a principal in a larger firm, ask for a history of the firm and some information on how the firm is run.

**Office Tour.** If appropriate, ask for a tour of the office. Hopefully you can be introduced to the lawyers and the members of the firm who would work on your matter. Make sure you are comfortable with the appearance of the offices. Pay attention to how the members of the firm interact with each other.

## 4.6   The Interview—How to Ask

Just as important as *what* you ask is *how* you ask questions, and listening to the answers is crucial.

**Follow an Outline.** Make an outline of the questions you want to ask before you go to see a lawyer for the first time. It's easy to get sidetracked by long answers or questions the lawyer asks you. An outline reduces the pressure to remember what you want to ask and gives you a place to take notes.

**Be Professional.** When dealing with any professional, you're more effective if you try to maintain a professional attitude and demeanor. What is a professional attitude? For starters, it isn't professional to try to act like a lawyer. To be professional and get the most from your time, focus on the issues you need to discuss. Don't spend your time talking about shared hobbies, friends or sports. The worst reason to hire a lawyer is that he likes the same sports you do. Try to avoid emotional outbursts or using your lawyer as a listening ear. Talk about the facts of the case, how your lawyer-client relationship would work, and how to get to an appropriate outcome. Be polite but firm.

If the lawyer does not appear to be answering a question, explain that you don't feel that the question was answered or that you didn't understand the response. You don't have to be rude, but you may have to repeat yourself. At some point in an interview, you may decide that this lawyer is *not* the one you want to hire. Try not to make an instant decision unless it's really clear.

**Open Questions.** Ask open-ended questions, ones that requires an answer that includes an explanation. A closed question is, "Did you go to law school?" The open question is, "Tell me about your education."

| CLOSED | OPEN |
|---|---|
| Have you handled this kind of case before? | What other problems like mine have you handled? |
| Are you successful representing clients? | What is your best result in a case like mine and why did it go so well? |
| Is the fact we both want to keep the dog going to be a problem? | Based on what we discussed, what issues do you think may be a problem? |

Open questions avoid yes and no answers and allow lawyers to discuss their thoughts and impressions. Most lawyers won't stop at just a *yes* or *no* answer in the interview process; they want to sell you on their abilities.

You want to watch the lawyer start to think about your problem. Open questions help you to see what they know and whether they're listening.

**Clarify.** Don't be afraid to ask questions to clarify the information you receive. If the lawyer uses words you're unfamiliar with, ask for explanations. If a response doesn't really answer your question, ask it again. If the lawyer doesn't know the answer, decide whether the information is necessary to your decision about hiring him and determine how the response can be communicated to you. Most lawyers are willing to talk a lot. Understanding what is being said is your responsibility.

**Take Notes.** Use your outline and write down the important points. Don't trust your memory to keep track of the information you get and your impressions. Notes are a good way to keep track of information and events through the whole case, so start doing so in the first interview.

**Follow up.** Sometimes you may leave the interview with unanswered questions, or after leaving the interview, you might think of questions you should have asked. For me, it's usually when I start the car. So, during your interview, be sure to ask the lawyer how to get responses to additional questions you may have.

I prefer e-mail, but some lawyers may want to talk again, in person or by telephone. Be sure to discuss the possibility of additional questions ahead of time and come to an agreement on how they'll be handled.

## 4.7  Lawyers to Avoid

**Rainmaker.** Unless you're rich or a buyer of legal services for an organization, you'll probably never meet the Rainmaker. The Rainmaker is the salesman for larger law firms. He's is charming, talented, and manages to bill every hour he spends with clients on the golf course. He attracts clients, wines and dines them, but performs little actual legal work. You're unlikely to meet a large firm's rainmaker—but it's important to know that some lawyers are more salesman than advocate. The ability to sell you on hiring the firm may not be an indication of great ability or expertise in finding a solution to your problem.

**Adverse Lawyers.** Avoid lawyers who appear desperate, greedy, or arrogant; these attributes are adverse to your interest in getting a good result. Some lawyers are one or all of these things, and choosing someone who rubs you the wrong way or doesn't have your best interests at heart isn't a good way to start a professional relationship. Lawyers who need your money, or the money you represent, promise everything now but later deliver as little as possible. Make sure you understand all of the ways your lawyer will bill you (see Chapter 5). Don't pay a retainer until it's clear that all the lawyers you interview will require a retainer. Avoid law firms that handle as many clients as possible unless you're sure that your work doesn't require special attention.

**Busy.** Steer clear of lawyers who are too busy. This is easier than it sounds; good lawyers are usually in demand and have lots of clients. But if your lawyer is handling too many matters, getting information to and from him will be difficult. You may not be able to develop the professional relationship you want. In some cases, you may have to accept that the primary lawyer is simply too busy to handle the day-to-day affairs of your problem, and, in fact, may only show up at trial. One of the most important things you want from your lawyer is the time you'll pay for, and a focus on communicating with you.

**Guarantees.** Lawyers are not supposed to guarantee a specific result, because they can't control the legal process. Be concerned about lawyers who are over-optimistic about their ability or promise a specific result. It's great to have a lawyer who is confident; the best lawyers are confident. A truly great lawyer will be able to demonstrate past success with your type of case, but he'll tell you that every case is different and that there are no guarantees. If a lawyer promises a specific result or outcome, ask for the promise in writing so you have proof if the result doesn't happen.

**Trust Yourself.** Above all, trust your intuition. When you take the time to meet several different lawyers, you'll begin to see how different they are, and, in some cases, how differently they'll approach your legal problem. If you talk to a lawyer and something doesn't feel right, move on. Whether your intuition is right or wrong is less important than starting your professional relationship with confidence. There is no perfect lawyer, but there are probably many lawyers who can do a good job and with whom you'll feel comfortable and enjoy working.

## 4.8   Making a Decision

Once the interviews are done, you need to make a decision. It should be based on the information you collected, your impressions of the lawyers and their firms, the cost of the different choices, and the value or importance of the outcome of the legal process.

Remember: you're hiring a lawyer to solve a legal problem. It's important to like your lawyer, but hiring a lawyer you like who gets a bad result doesn't make sense.

**Timing.** Don't let the decision drag out. When you have talked to all of the lawyers, make a decision. Confirm to your choice that he's been hired and let the other interviewees know that you've made a decision.

**Communication.** After you hire your lawyer, follow up in writing. Write your understanding of the scope of the relationship: the nature of the problem, the cost of handling the matter, and anything else that was discussed during or after the interview. This helps to make sure that everyone is on the same page and that there are no misunderstandings regarding your retention of the lawyer.

**Confirmation.** Ask your lawyer to confirm the retention and his plan of action. Get confirmation of what is expected of you and how the process will begin. If payment is a contingent fee agreement, your lawyer will have to provide you with a written summary of the fee agreement. Most lawyers will have you sign a retention letter. See Chapter 5 for an explanation of contingent fee agreements and when you might be able to negotiate a better fee.

**Documentation.** Keep copies of everything you send your lawyer and all of the letters and e-mails you receive. Save everything from the beginning and continue until your legal matter is resolved. Keep everything organized so you can find documents when you need them. See Chapter 11 for suggestions on how to organize the documents you'll receive.

# 5. The Lawyer's Fee—How You Pay

*"A lawyer starts life giving $500 worth of law for $5
and ends giving $5 worth for $500."*
Benjamin H. Brewster

Saving money is important to most clients, but money saved in the cost of a lawyer may be lost in the outcome of the case. Whether you have a civil matter that involves large sums of money or a criminal case that could result in losing a significant portion of your life, be willing to spend the time it takes to find the right lawyer. When you find him, be willing to spend the money necessary to engage him.

On the other hand, you can spend too much money on a case. It's easy to spend large sums on lawyers without getting the result you want. Don't let the lawyers become the only winners in your dispute.

Read the bills you receive. Understand how you're being charged for legal services. Be willing to ask questions about bills. Expect bills to be adjusted or reduced when it's appropriate.

## 5.1   Financial Advantage?

So what do you want? There are a number of things to look for when hiring a lawyer, but the most important is a solution to your legal problem. Many clients get so involved in the legal soap opera that they forget there's actually a goal. Initially, the goal is to win, but the reality of most cases reduces that goal to finding a solution that makes sense and that everyone can live with. So, as you attempt to solve your legal problems, here are some factors to be considered when deciding how much you are willing to pay your lawyer.

---
**Lawyer-Client Rule Number 5**

Stay focused on the legal problem and the best possible outcome. Don't get lost in the side battles or control expenses to the detriment of your result.

---

**Efficiency**. When hiring an experienced lawyer, you should be getting someone who's done this work before and doesn't need to do as much research or recreate his legal education. If your lawyer and his office have handled hundreds of cases just like yours, this should be an advantage. An experienced lawyer shouldn't charge for basic research or documents that have already been created. This isn't just a matter of money—it is a violation of ethical rules. When you pay for legal work, make sure it's for real time. If the lawyer has to do research to understand the basic law in your case or to create basic legal documents, negotiate a lower hourly rate.

**Expertise.** Expertise is like efficiency in many ways, but it also implies that you're paying for an increased chance of a better outcome. For example, picture two law firms who handle divorce cases where both firms are very efficient. One has developed special expertise in finding hidden assets or money. Both firms are efficient, but if you suspect that a soon to be ex-spouse has hidden money, you need that specific expertise.

**Energy and Commitment.** Sometimes the right lawyer for your legal problem is not one who has experience or expertise, but a lawyer who is hungry for work and willing to pay extra attention to you. As a sophisticated buyer of legal services I love young, hungry lawyers looking to develop a reputation. They're willing to work extra hard to keep clients happy and they really want to win.

**Outcome.** Beware of the lawyer who promises that he'll win your case. Even great lawyers lose. Don't ask a lawyer to be unethical for you. Lawyers who break the rules cause huge problems for clients who usually bear the consequences of an angry judge or sanctions for a lawyer's actions or unethical recommendations. On the other hand, good lawyers consistently get outstanding results and have a reputation for excellence in representing clients.

## 5.2 Set Expectations

When you hire a lawyer, one of the biggest questions you have is how much it'll cost. There are times when cost really is no object, but they're rare. What is more common is that anticipated high costs cause people to not seek legal advice.

During your interviews (Chapter 4), one of the questions you asked was, "How much will this cost?" You asked the lawyers to explain how they'll bill for their time and the anticipated costs of your matter. The next question you need to ask is almost as important and may help you understand the time frame your case will take: "*Why* will it cost this much?"

Your lawyer is probably unable to give you an exact cost of the case, so you have to be flexible. You'll need to understand several things.

First, how is your lawyer actually paid. See the following sections for descriptions of how lawyers arrange to get paid and make sure you understand the costs you'll be required to pay and when.

Second, the steps required to handle your legal problem. Ask your lawyer to outline the basic procedural steps required and how much time and money each of these steps will take. If your legal problem involves big issues that will be energetically contested by the other side, it'll be harder anticipating just how much time and money it will take. By the same token, if you ask your lawyer to fight every possible battle that comes up, the case will cost more.

If the work you need is fairly standard and there are no hidden issues or confrontations, your lawyer should be able to give you a good idea of how much it'll cost. Get an estimate of total costs as part of your first letter of representation. Ask your lawyer to let you know if he's going to exceed the budget and why. If you request additional legal services get an estimate of the additional costs.

Third, question unusual costs or time spent on your matter that weren't discussed or seem out of the ordinary. See the list below for some of the types of costs that are appropriate and examples of costs that can be questioned.

| APPROPRIATE | QUESTIONABLE |
| --- | --- |
| 1. Hourly fees for lawyers and paralegals. | 1. Fees for secretaries or support staff. |
| 2. Fees related to filing legal documents in court. | 2. Fees for preparing documents—typing pool or transcription fees. |
| 3. Expert fees. | 3. Fees for overhead items—long distance calls, normal postage, or the cost of online research services. |
| 4. Travel expenses for lawyers on pre-approved travel. | |

## 5.3   The Hourly Fee

The hourly fee is the most common way to pay for legal services. It's when the lawyer charges an hourly rate for the time spent working on your problem. Depending on the part of the country, the type of law, and the experience of the lawyer, fees can range from $50 to $1,000 an hour. Hourly rates tend to be higher in bigger cities and for senior partners in bigger law firms.

Your lawyer should be very clear about what his fee is and the hourly rate of any other members of the firm who may work on your file. Request a summary, in writing, of all of the other costs that you may be charged. It's not unreasonable to be charged for actual costs incurred by your lawyer, including special mail costs, copying costs, court filing fees and the cost of outside resources like experts.

You should *not* be paying for expenses like secretarial time, long distance charges, or fees for setting up your file; these are internal costs, and the hourly rate should cover them. If your lawyer insists on charging you for them, find another lawyer. Don't be afraid to dispute unexpected costs or ones that seem excessive.

The biggest advantage of hourly fees is that it's easy to compare the costs of two different lawyers; and in theory, you only pay for the time spent.

The hourly fee has significant disadvantages as well. When your lawyer is being paid by the hour, it's to his advantage for the case to drag on. Lawyers tend to be methodical in handling legal work, so when they're paid by the hour, they have little incentive to find efficient ways to handle cases or to seek early resolution.

Another disadvantage is that lawyers don't always work every minute they charge for. The image of a lawyer padding his bill is a cliché, but unfortunately it still happens. I've known lawyers who regularly billed twenty-six-hour days.

The most common type of bill inflation occurs when a lawyer charges you by the hour but uses a set rate for tasks that take less time to accomplish. A common example is preparing a lawsuit or a response to a pleading. A lawyer might bill for a set amount of time even though they used a template or had an employee do the work.

It's all right—and even necessary—for a lawyer to charge a reasonable fee for his work, but if you're paying for his time you should be billed for his time. If your lawyer has years of experience, you're probably paying a higher hourly rate; you shouldn't pay for the time it took the lawyer to create his first response.

It can be very difficult to prove that your lawyer is padding his bill or charging for things that he didn't actually do. But there are some things you can do to help prevent blatant fraud.

Ask for monthly, detailed bills. Review your bills carefully. If the charges don't have detail or descriptions, ask your lawyer to provide them. Confirm the time and length of conversations you had with your lawyer to the billing detail. Evaluate descriptions and the described tasks; don't be afraid to dispute unreasonable amounts, like being billed .3 of an hour or 18 minutes for a one-sentence email.

If the lawyer seems to have spent a long time reading a document or doing research, ask for the document or the notes from his research. You have the right to get enough information to confirm that your lawyer is looking out for your best interests. On the other hand, don't become so demanding that you destroy the professional relationship. In the end, if you don't trust your lawyer, you should seriously consider getting another one.

Every time you call your lawyer or ask him to do something for you, you'll be billed for that time. Whenever you meet with your lawyer you'll be billed. Every time you ask him to handle something else you'll be billed. When a lawyer sells his time for money he's willing to sell all you want—and the fees can add up quickly.

## 5.4   The Contingency Fee

A contingency fee is one paid from the final proceeds of a case. Most common in personal injury litigation, the contingency fee is paid only if the lawyer prevails in the case, and then he takes a percentage of the final settlement or judgment as his fee.

Most states limit the types of cases where a contingency fee is allowed. For example, lawyers aren't allowed to take a percentage of a divorce case settlement as a fee. Ironically, you may have to sell your house to pay the legal bills, but your lawyer can't negotiate a fee that requires you to pay him a percentage of what you get from the divorce.

Some states also limit the percentages a lawyer can take in any given case. These states require the lawyer to disclose that he can only take a certain percentage of the proceeds of the case, although that percentage may change depending on how far the case proceeds.

The contingency fee is appealing to many clients. Since personal injury cases are often risky, and there's a chance you won't collect any money, some people are hesitant to pursue a case if they have to pay costs up front. Contingency fees also ensure that lawyers are honest about your chances of prevailing in the case, since they don't want to invest a lot of time and effort in a bad case.

However, there are downsides to contingency fees as well. The biggest one is that a contingency fee will reduce the money you receive. Many clients are surprised when they finally receive their portion of the payment. Few clients understand that the costs of pursuing the case are *in addition to* the lawyer's fee. For example, if you sign a contingency fee agreement that says the lawyer gets forty percent of the amount received, costs will be taken out first. You may actually receive less than half the settlement or judgment.

Many states require a lawyer to inform clients that only the fee is contingent and that the client is responsible for the costs even if the lawyer loses. However, this rule is often ignored and personal injury firms often absorb these costs as part of doing business. While this may be a breach of ethical rules, it's one that benefits clients who are already upset that they lost their case. Lawyers don't get in trouble because clients never complain when they don't have to pay expenses.

Contingency fees are used in almost all personal injury cases, even when it doesn't benefit the client. Lawyers who handle personal injury cases justify the universal use of contingent fees by claiming it allows them to represent clients who cannot otherwise afford a lawyer. But if there is clear liability and substantial damages it may make more sense for the client to hire a lawyer on an hourly basis instead of paying a huge percentage of the settlement.

Good personal injury lawyers don't take high-risk cases; they make good money in contingency fees because they only take cases that will result in significant damages being paid.

In some cases, lawyers use a sliding scale for their contingent fee. The lawyer (in addition to the costs of the case) gets twenty percent of the money if it can be settled before filing a lawsuit, thirty percent if the case is filed but is settled before trial, and forty percent if the case goes to a jury. The upside for the client is that the fee is less if the case is resolved early; the downside is that lawyers are incentivized to drag out the resolution.

When hiring a lawyer with a contingency fee arrangement, make sure you understand both how the fee arrangement works and how the costs will be handled. Ask if an hourly rate is possible and what it would cost. Ask for an outline of the costs of preparing the case. Even if your state doesn't require a sliding contingency fee schedule, see if the lawyer will agree to a more flexible fee arrangement.

Understand whether your lawyer's percentage is taken from the **gross** or **net** settlement. Most settlements are not for millions of dollars. If the lawyer's percentage is based on the gross settlement it'll be a higher amount because the gross includes the costs of the case.

See what happens on a $100,000 settlement with a 40% contingent fee and $25,000 in costs.

| Fee from Gross Settlement | Fee From Net Settlement |
|---|---|
| $100,000 Settlement | $100,000 Settlement |
| Less Fee (40% of $100,000): $40,000 | Less Costs: $25,000 |
| Less Costs: $25,000 | Less Fee (40% of $75,000): $30,000 |
| Total to Client: $35,000 | Total to Client: $45,000 |

**Alternate Contingent Fees**. You could try to negotiate different arrangements, for instance, mixing fee methods. A lawyer might agree to a lower hourly rate combined with a smaller contingent fee. For example, if the lawyer normally charges either $200 an hour or a thirty percent contingency fee for your type of case, offer to pay $100 dollars an hour for his time and ten percent of the final settlement.

A mixed fee arrangement has the advantage of allowing you to monitor the work as it's being done; with a contingency fee you wouldn't receive bills. This also ensures the lawyer payment for his time and provides an incentive to maximize your recovery.

Another possible method, which unfortunately most lawyers won't be excited about, is to negotiate a fee based on a percentage of how much the lawyer can collect for you beyond what you can get without him.

For example, if you're hurt in an auto accident and the other driver was at fault you can contact the other driver's insurance company and see what they will pay for your injuries. This is what you can collect without involving a lawyer. Take the offer to a lawyer and agree to pay him a contingent fee of anything he can collect over the offer. Make sure you don't sign any documents from the other driver's insurer or lawyer without getting advice from your lawyer. This method works best in big damage cases where the other side wants to get the dispute resolved and a good lawyer can maximize your recovery.

Another contingent fee alternative to consider is a reverse sliding percentage, where the percentage goes down as the settlement or recovery gets bigger. This kind of arrangement is sometimes used in the large damage cases. The lawyer collects a regular percentage or fee up to a certain amount, and then gets a lower percentage after that. For example, a lawyer might get 40% of a settlement up to $500,000. Then his percentage drops to 10% after that.

Top lawyers argue that this creates a disincentive to work for a bigger settlement but having a lawyer make millions from a case without any limits doesn't benefit the client. You'll know if you have a large damage case because of the significant costs and damages to you and the number of lawyers wanting to represent you.

## 5.5   The Retainer

Retainers are common for business clients and first-time clients. Two types of retainer agreements are used by lawyers today: the traditional retention-retainer agreement and the fee-reducing retainer agreement.

**Retention Retainers** are a fee paid for the right to retain and use a specific lawyer or law firm. They require the client to pay a set fee for the exclusive right to use the lawyer or firm for a specific period of time. The retainer is not usually applied to the actual fee you'll pay when the lawyer starts working on your problem. Instead, it's a negotiated price of a promise that the lawyer will handle that type of work for you exclusively. When you actually need the lawyer, then you'll start paying the negotiated hourly fee.

If you know that during the next year you'll need a lawyer to handle several similar cases, you may agree to pay a retainer to ensure that the best lawyer for that kind of law is always available to handle your work.

**Fee-Reducing Retainers** are more common. They require you to pay a certain sum up front that is applied to your legal fees and costs. This is usually to protect the lawyer from the risk of not being paid and is very common when you are the sole source of payment and there are no future monetary awards from your case; as in a criminal defense case. A modification of this type of agreement is a security-deposit retainer that is held by the firm until the case is over and all fees paid. At that point, the retainer is returned to the client.

The typical fee-reducing retainer agreement requires payment of a specific amount before the lawyer will starts working; often $20,000 or more. The lawyer will provide you a regular accounting of what is being billed and how much money is left. After a certain amount of money has been used the lawyer may have the right to ask that more money be put into the account.

The purpose of this kind of agreement is to protect the lawyer. It can be difficult for a lawyer to stop handling a case once he has started, even if he's not being paid. This way they have most of the expected costs before they start an official client relationship. A law firm that requires a retainer won't represent you until they receive it.

As with any billing agreement, make sure that your retainer agreement is in writing. The contract should set out the duties of both parties and include information such as the hourly rates the lawyer is charging, how costs will be handled and how long the agreement will last.

The retainer agreement may be the best source of documentation of what you intended when you hired your lawyer, so make sure it includes all your agreements and understanding of what your lawyer is going to do as well as any information on how he is going to do it.

## 5.6 The Fixed Fee

The fixed fee is a set price for a specific legal service. It is also known as a flat fee. Common examples are paying a set price for a will, a simple trust or to form a corporation. Fixed fees are useful for small legal projects, but they can also be used for bigger ones if both sides have a good understanding of the legal work that needs to be done.

For example, an apartment owner who needs a lawyer to deal with contract issues or evict renters for non-payment. If the owner knows that the average cost of a contract is $1,000, it may make more sense just to agree to pay $1,000 for every case he sends the lawyer rather than receive and pay legal bills every month. Often clients will try to negotiate a discount if the fee is paid in advance. Instead of paying

$1,000, the owner may offer the lawyer $900 per case, with the money paid when the case is started rather than at the end.

When hiring a lawyer to handle a single case there probably won't be an opportunity to pay a fixed fee and there's a good chance you wouldn't know what a fair fee is.

Fixed fees work best when you have regular work and multiple cases with the same firm. The advantage to you is knowing what the cost will be. Another potential advantage is that a lawyer being paid to get a job done tends to be more efficient and work faster than a lawyer charging by the hour.

A disadvantage of the fixed fee can be getting your lawyer to spend as much time as you think your case needs. The fixed fee can be a good way to pay for legal services, but for the lawyer to be motivated and attentive both the client and the lawyer need to know what needs to be done, and there has to be an ongoing relationship with regular work.

## 5.7  Things to Remember

**Always take the time to understand how you are paying your lawyer.** Misunderstandings about how a lawyer will be paid—and how much a case will cost—are the biggest causes of arguments and problems in the lawyer-client relationship. Always try to understand how billing is done and what is expected of you as a client.

If you're using a contingency fee agreement, ask your lawyer for examples of how much the fee will be if you settle the claim or go to trial. Don't be afraid to ask about alternatives to the proposed fee arrangement.

**Get everything in writing.** Don't sign a "standard" contract if you believe that what you're agreeing to is different from what's written. Look at the whole agreement reading all of the addendums and small print, because they can have a huge impact on what you pay. If someone has to resolve a dispute between you and your lawyer the written and signed contract will win over any other discussions you had. The contract or agreement should be easily understood and should be what you agreed to.

**Resolve problems quickly.** When an issue comes up get it resolved quickly. If you dispute a specific bill call your lawyer immediately and get it resolved. If you're going to have trouble paying your legal bills let your lawyer know as soon as possible. Will he withdraw? Maybe, but it's better to discuss the issue before you get to a crucial point and he loses interest because of unpaid bills.

**Understand the cost.** One of the biggest advantages of dealing with a lawyer who lets you know the cost of your representation is that you can make an informed decision on whether it makes sense to hire a lawyer in the first place.

A potential client wanted me to help to sue his neighbor because of a long- standing argument over the boundary line between their properties. After reviewing the problem I recommended he either try to get along with his neighbor or move. I pointed out that what he really wanted was to escalate the fight. It would be much better use of his money to sell and find a dream house with new neighbors, a larger yard and a clear boundary.

He didn't hire me—which was great!

# 6. The Professional Relationship

*"A lawyer is a person who writes a 10,000-word document and calls it a 'brief.'"*
Franz Kafka

## 6.1  The Attorney-Client Relationship:

When a client hires a lawyer, a special relationship is created. This relationship is defined by tradition, by law, and by special rules called the lawyer's code of ethics. The code of ethics is the standard that lawyers are supposed to follow when practicing law and especially when representing individual clients.

Section 6.3 briefly outlines the model rules. A client should be aware that these rules exist, what they cover, and that your lawyer has an obligation imposed by the state.

No list can cover every detail of a professional relationship with a lawyer. It's important to remember that you're hiring a lawyer to accomplish something for you—to achieve a specific outcome in a legal situation or problem you have. While liking your lawyer is a good start, it may be even better to find the lawyer who gives you the best chance of getting a good legal result for the right cost. When you choose your lawyer, even if you don't become best friends, you have a right to expect the following professional behaviors.

**Respect and Courtesy.** A lawyer who demeans your opinions, is insulting, or fails to exercise professional courtesy is a huge problem. Lawyers can be arrogant, and many lawyers—especially good ones—have large egos. While you want a lawyer who believes he is the best at what he does, ego is not an excuse for a lawyer to act unprofessionally.

**Competence and Diligence.** The most frequent mistake made by lawyers is missing case deadlines. Your lawyer must be honest about his ability to handle your legal work; he has a responsibility to file documents within the required time limits and let you know if deadlines are missed.

While the normal pace of the legal system can be frustrating to a client, sometimes lawyers drag out cases. That may be because they want to bill more hours, but usually it's because they have a number of matters coming up at the same time. Make sure your lawyer lets you know when he asks for a time extension or delays a legal process. If the delay is for a good reason your lawyer should be able to explain it; but if your lawyer makes a regular practice of delaying your matter you need more information so you can evaluate his handling of your case.

**Focus on the Client.** A lawyer is supposed to use his best professional judgment on your behalf. He should not make decisions based on how your problems will affect his personal interests or the interests of his other clients.

Lawyers are being unethical when they fail to represent a client vigorously for money or because it would harm other clients. If a lawyer has a conflict between the interests or desires of different clients, those clients need to know about it. Lawyers can and will have many clients at the same time, but each one should feel secure that the lawyer is looking out for him or her as if they were the only client.

**Reasonable Fee.** A lawyer's fee should be reasonable, and he should be able to explain in advance how that fee will be computed. See Chapter 5 for more information on how lawyers are paid. Not only is it good practice for a lawyer to explain his fee, but he has an ethical responsibility to do so. What is "reasonable" depends on the geographic area, the reputation and experience of the lawyer and his firm, and the type of case. For some work $50 an hour is reasonable. For other work and other lawyers $1,000 an hour is reasonable.

Reasonableness can also depend on how efficient a lawyer is. A client isn't better off picking a lawyer who charges a little less but takes twice as long to do the work.

**Prompt and Professional Response.** Your lawyer, not his or her paralegal or secretary, should always respond quickly to telephone calls and written communications from you. When you have a question your lawyer should be able to answer it, especially if it's about a bill or the status of your file. Some questions require research, but your lawyer should still be responsive in a reasonable amount of time.

**Regular Updates.** Your lawyer should keep you informed about the status of your case. This includes staying in contact, providing you updates, and copying you on important papers. You have a right to get copies of the documents your lawyer creates on your behalf, like pleadings or memos.

**Client Confidence.** You have a right to expect your lawyer to preserve client confidences by keeping information learned during the lawyer-client relationship private and confidential. One of the most important aspects of a lawyer-client relationship is that the lawyer is supposed to keep your secrets.

This privilege has existed for hundreds of years and is there to allow a lawyer and his client to talk about anything in a case without fear that the lawyer will become a witness against his client. This is one of the most important ethical obligations that a lawyer has, and violating this trust will usually result in the lawyer losing his right to practice law.

Remember that some documents, like letters or opinions, are confidential. If you share them with others you may lose the ability to keep them confidential.

**Honesty.** You should expect your lawyer to deal honestly and truthfully with you, other lawyers, and the judge. Lawyers have an ethical obligation to tell the truth in professional matters. It would make sense to want your lawyer to always tell you the truth and the court feels the same way.

A judge will sometimes punish both the lawyer and the client if a lawyer lies to the judge. Sometimes lawyers don't want to know everything from a client, like whether he committed a crime, because once a lawyer knows the truth he can't lie to the court or allow his client to lie. Most lawyers take this responsibility very seriously, although some lawyers are willing to bend the truth more than a little to win a case.

It's important for you to make sure that your lawyer is honest with everyone. A lawyer willing to lie to the judge on your behalf will probably lie to you if it suits his needs.

**Not Abusing the System.** Sometimes clients want their lawyers to be a hired gun. They want to hurt their opponent, using the legal system to get revenge or to punish. The law—and those who work in the law—have a responsibility to seek legal solutions, not revenge.

**Respect.** You should expect your lawyer to respect your decisions as long as they are permitted by law and the rules of professional conduct, including whether to settle. At some point, you may have to make a decision to end a legal fight such as in cases where it doesn't make sense to keep going, whether it's costing too much money or you don't want to "roll the dice" and risk everything on what a jury decides. These are your decisions. An ethical lawyer will explain your choices and the consequences and will then respect your right to make these decisions.

## 6.2   What Your Lawyer Expects from You

Your lawyer has the right to expect certain things of you. The lawyer-client relationship is a two-way street, and without your help and direction the lawyer will find it very difficult to get to a solution that's right for you. An ethical lawyer will expect the following from a good client.

**The Truth.** A lawyer can't help you if he isn't sure whether you're telling him the truth. Nothing is worse for a lawyer than to be surprised when the other side proves that a client has lied about the facts or circumstances of a legal dispute.

Your lawyer needs to know both the good and bad things about a case. Forget about impressing your lawyer; he's not the jury. If he doesn't know the truth he can't evaluate your options and represent your interests. Always tell your lawyer the truth. Remember that he has to keep everything that you tell him confidential. Good lawyers will usually fire clients who lie to them.

---
**Lawyer-Client Rule Number 6**

Always tell your lawyer the truth. Your lawyer needs to know the good and the bad facts. Your lawyer cannot tell anyone your secrets, but he needs to know all the facts.

---

**Courtesy and Respect.** Some clients think that because they are paying their lawyer, that there's no need to treat him with common courtesy. In my experience, these are usually the clients who have the most problems paying bills on time.

Rude behavior, impossible demands, and abusive conduct will not get your lawyer to perform better, faster or cheaper. In fact, it will have the opposite effect. Being a rude or high-maintenance client will always cost you more in the end, whether in fees or in the outcome.

**Notification of Changes in Your Circumstances.** If you move, make a major life change, or desire a different outcome, please let your lawyer know.

**Respect Your Lawyer's Time.** Good lawyers have many clients who are equally deserving of their time and efforts. Always make an appointment if you need to meet with your lawyer. Telephone calls are usually more effective and helpful if you schedule a time to talk on the telephone rather than calling out of the blue.

I was always more prepared to talk to a client if I could pull their file and have the information I needed on my desk before a call. In these situations, clients were always happier because I could answer their questions quickly and the call didn't take as much time or cost as much money. E-mail is a great tool for staying in contact with your lawyer or setting up a call.

**Quick Responses to Requests.** In most civil legal proceedings, the people involved in the case will have to provide information and documents related to the case. Don't hide documents. Always provide the information as quickly as possible. If you don't understand what is being asked for, look to your lawyer to help you understand. Not providing information needed by your lawyer or that has been requested by the other side can cause you to lose.

**Be on Time.** If you lawyer tells you that you have to be at court or come to his office at a certain time for a process or meeting, be there. Your lawyer will do his best to work with you to set dates and times that work best for you. You need to be at proceedings when requested by your lawyer. You also need to follow your lawyer's instructions on how to dress, because looking appropriate can be important in a trial or in front of the judge.

**Communicate.** Do not let frustrations build up. If your legal matter isn't going in the right direction or you don't understand what's happening, let your lawyer know. A good lawyer will work with you to make matters right or help you understand what's happening in the process. Lawyers expect their clients to have anxiety about being part of a legal process. For most clients it can be an intimidating process and not communicating with your lawyer can make it worse.

**No Illegal or Unethical Requests.** Lawyers can fire clients for only a few reasons, one of them is being asked to do something illegal or unethical.

**Pay Bills Promptly.** One of the other reasons a lawyer can fire clients is if they have stopped paying for legal services. The lawyer makes his living by selling his time or solutions to legal problems. The rules of ethics allow a lawyer to stop representing clients not honoring their promise to pay. If you have questions regarding your bills, talk to your lawyer; don't stop paying your bills. If you can no longer afford to pay, be sure to talk to your lawyer immediately and see if something can be worked out.

## 6.3 The Rules of Ethics

Each state has a set of ethical rules usually called the Rules or Code of Professional Conduct. While there are differences from state to state, most of these rules follow the same format and accomplish the same objectives. The basic format, or model rules, were developed by the American Bar Association (the "ABA") and are revised on a regular basis.

While only a few states have adopted the model rules as written, most follow the basic structure of the Model Rules and consider recommended changes by the ABA.

For a lawyer, the rules are an import guide to the professional relationship. They're usually enforced by the supreme court in each state and when you complain to a state bar about something a lawyer has done, they're used to determine whether an ethical rule was broken.

The Model Rules are divided into eight sections.

**Section 1: The Lawyer-Client Relationship.** This section deals with the heart of a lawyer's obligations towards a client. It requires a lawyer to be diligent, competent, charge a fair fee, and protect current and past clients. Much of it sets out the rules for avoiding conflicts between different clients, or a conflict of interest. The rules exist to prevent a lawyer from causing harm to a client he has agreed to represent by taking another case with a different client with an opposite interest. For example, if your lawyer were asked to take a case on behalf of a new client—who wants to sue you. Because you've shared personal information with your lawyer and your lawyer knows information that can be used against you, your lawyer cannot agree to take a case opposing you.

**Section 2. The Lawyer as a Counselor.** This section gives guidance to lawyers in their obligation to not just be an advocate, but also to give legal advice and help clients understand their options and the possible outcomes of their choices. It allows a lawyer to discuss factors other than the law, for example, "moral, economic, social and political factors," when helping a client to make decisions.

**Section 3. The Lawyer as an Advocate.** An advocate is someone who champions your cause and tries to convince others that you should win your dispute. Most lawyers are great at being enthusiastic advocates and the rules are there to define the boundaries of their behavior. This section requires that lawyers pursue only meritorious claims and only take positions that are justified by the law. Lawyers have an obligation to be honest with the court, with opposing parties, and with other lawyers.

**Section 4. Dealing with People Who Are not Clients.** There are guidelines set for lawyers dealing with people who aren't clients. Examples include opposing parties, witnesses, and potential clients. Generally lawyers should be honest and show professional respect toward people who aren't their clients. Lawyers also have special guidelines for dealing with people represented by other lawyers. They have an obligation to contact the other lawyer rather than communicate directly with the person he represents.

**Section 5: Law Firms and Associations.** Here, rules have to do with ethical issues related to running a law firm and the responsibility of partners to be accountable for the associates and staff in a firm.

**Section 6: Public Service.** Lawyers are expected to perform some form of public service, including taking cases without a fee or serving clients when appointed by a court. This section outlines lawyers' responsibilities to accept court-assigned clients and the responsibilities of the lawyer when working with community organizations or advocating change in the legal system.

**Section 7. Information About Legal Services.** This section sets guidelines on what methods of advertising are considered professional and what representations lawyers can make when advertising their legal services and abilities. Historically, most states had strict rules about what kinds of advertising lawyers could do, but those rules were challenged and now more liberal advertising, including radio and TV ads, is allowed. Strict restrictions still remain, however, on what kind of contact a lawyer is supposed to have with potential clients who haven't contacted them. Most states prohibit or discourage lawyers from actively trying to solicit clients, a guideline sometimes ignored by aggressive lawyers.

**Section 8. The Integrity of the Profession.** This section deals with admission to practice law, rules regarding courts, misconduct by lawyers and disciplinary action against lawyers.

## 6.4 What the Ethical Lawyer Can't Do

Some lawyers don't always act ethically. Sometime clients prefer lawyers who are willing to bend the rules for their benefit, but these same clients are often surprised when a lack of ethics extends to their relationship with their own lawyer. If you want to find a lawyer willing to win at any cost you're on your own. Be warned that ethics protect both the integrity of the legal system and the client—you.

Assuming that you're looking for a lawyer who has integrity and will represent you within the rules, here are some things that your lawyer *cannot* do.

**Lie for a client or allow the client to lie.** Lawyers should take seriously the oaths and statements made in the legal process. When a witness is called to testify they take an oath, and lawyers have an obligation to make sure that the truth is told.

One of the keys to being a good lawyer is helping your client answer only the question being asked. If the question is well-asked and the answer is clear then the truth needs to be given. The courts rely on clients, witnesses and lawyers to tell the truth to ensure that the system works.

Lawyers are officers of the court. This means that they have taken an oath to work within the boundaries of the legal system and to uphold the law and the ethical rules. Even though lawyers have a bad reputation regarding telling the truth, my experience is that most lawyers are ethical and won't lie for a client or knowingly allow a client to lie under oath.

**Wage war.** The purpose of the civil legal system is to resolve disputes. Lawyers have an obligation to be an advocate for their client, but they also have ethical responsibilities to the legal system and to society as a whole.

In order to keep within the boundaries of these sometimes conflicting responsibilities, the ethical rules allow a lawyer to be concerned first about his client but not to use the law as a weapon to punish someone else. In legal disputes emotions can run high and the parties often want more than mere money or possession of property;

they want their pound of flesh. An ethical lawyer has an obligation to seek remedies allowed under the law and to not use the legal system inappropriately.

Legal wars often occur when the parties lose sight of what they wanted in the first place, whether it was getting out of a bad marriage, resolving a business relationship gone bad, or collecting damages for an injury. The conflict takes on a life of its own and inflicting harm becomes the new goal. Everything is a fight and every action by the opposition is seen as a personal attack.

In these cases the clients forget that they wanted resolution and lawyers, who charge by the hour, are only too willing to drag things out. An ethical lawyer is not only is an advocate but is also a counselor who takes the time to help a client keep focused on the result and not become wrapped up in the "battle" of the legal system.

**Win every time.** No lawyer can win every case. There are great cases, and there are poor cases. With every new client I'd evaluate which side of the case I would like to have if I could choose. If I would rather have the other side's case, I'd let my client know that.

Sometimes it doesn't matter if the odds are against you, but there are times you need to know that the law or the facts are not in your favor and an ethical lawyer will tell you so. The decision to go forward is still yours and unless pursuing your case violates ethical rules your lawyer will do so with all of his skill and ability.

Some cases are great for a lawyer and his client, but no case is a 100% sure winner. Keep in mind that while *you* have everything to lose your lawyer has much less at stake. Good people with good cases who have turned down good resolutions sometimes receive nothing when the jury comes back.

Your lawyer will not win every case. Are you willing to bet everything that you'll win?

## 6.5  The Insurance Defense Lawyer

When you are sued by someone who has suffered an injury and you have insurance that covers the event or the alleged damages, your insurance company will usually hire a lawyer to represent you and defend you in the case. This type of relationship is a unique three-party relationship between you, the lawyer and the insurance company. You are the client, but the insurance company has money at risk in the event of a verdict against you. They also have a relationship with the lawyer who has been hired, because they hired him and will be paying the bills.

Having a lawyer hired by an insurance company is usually a great thing. The insurance company knows experienced lawyers and gives out a lot of business, which means they are a sophisticated buyer and have professionals supervising the legal process. In addition, since the insurance company has the most at stake if you lose, they want to successfully defend you.

The downside of this relationship is that the lawyers know who they need to keep happy if they want to get more business—and it's not you. You'll probably never use an insurance defense lawyer again, but the insurance company can keep them busy for a career.

If there's a dispute between you and your insurance company, the lawyer they hired cannot help you at all. Disputes can be about a variety of things, but the most common ones involve insurance coverage for the claims, For example, if you don't have enough insurance to cover the possible damages or when you want a different outcome than your insurance company. In these cases, you'll probably have to hire another lawyer—not to defend the lawsuit, but to help resolve your disputes with the insurance company.

You can do a couple of things to make sure you get great representation from a lawyer hired for you:

- Stay involved. Resist the temptation to stay out of the way and wait for the phone call that your case has been resolved.
- Ask to be copied on all of the documents and emails sent to the insurance company.
- Schedule regular phone calls, perhaps once a month, to discuss what's happening in the case.
- Ask your lawyer to let you know immediately if the insurance company makes a decision contrary to his recommendations or that

isn't in your best interest. While this is often a difficult decision by the lawyer, making this request in writing will help protect you if something bad happens in the case.

- Ask to receive copies of all legal bills sent to the insurance company. Even though you aren't paying them, you have a right to review them and make sure they're accurate. The bills can be a good source of information on what is happening in the case.
- If you're uncomfortable with your lawyer or you lack confidence in his ability, ask for another lawyer. With most insurance you can't choose the lawyer, but if you have serious concerns you can ask your insurance company to get you another one.

## 6.6   The Lawyer's Ethical Obligations

A lawyer has an obligation to act within the rules of ethics, which not only set limits on what he can do for his client but also what he cannot do. The rules do not—and do not try to—answer every question or deal with every situation. Within the rules there are many very different ways of practicing law and resolving legal problems. The key to a successful legal relationship is finding that mix of ethics, ability and attention you need and that your legal problem requires.

The ethical rules are designed to protect the client and the reputation of the legal community. Your lawyer should take the rules seriously, because his license to practice law is a privilege that can be taken away. The rules not only protect you, but they protect our legal system and its ability to resolve disputes.

# 7. The Lawyer's Job

*"Lawyers spend a great deal of their time shoveling smoke."*
Justice Oliver Wendell Holmes, Jr.

## 7.1 What the Lawyer Does Every Day

A lawyer's day is usually filled with many different activities, including meeting with new or existing clients, legal research, writing documents, or appearing in court. These activities will vary according to the type of law practice and the size and nature of the firm. A lawyer's activities can also depend on his position at the firm. A junior associate will spend more time doing legal research and handling routine court appearances than the senior partner who meets with clients and handles trials and finishes important documents.

While not a complete list of what lawyers do, the following descriptions will help illustrate some of the common tasks that most lawyers perform on a regular basis.

**Meeting with Clients.** Meeting with existing and potential clients can take up much of a lawyer's time. Associates may not spend a lot of time dealing with clients, but for partners it can be a daily event. These meetings ensure future work and are the end result of the firm's marketing efforts.

Lawyers meet with clients for a variety of reasons. In some meetings the lawyer reports on the case and up-coming events. In others, lawyers may meet with clients to prepare them for future events like trial or a deposition. Lawyers want to prepare clients for these event, sometimes for hours, to help them be as prepared as possible.

Lawyers will often meet to review legal documents from a case and get signatures or information. This is especially true of cases where discovery documents need to be given to the other side.

**Legal Research.** Legal research is something lawyers do. Every legal problem is different and requires study of the law and previous court cases. Research is also required when preparing documents for a case in litigation. Some types of legal work are mostly research. For instance, a lawyer specializing in patent law can spend a lot of time searching for similar patents when preparing to file a new application. Experience is the key to effective legal research, both in terms of doing it well and doing it quickly. Unfortunately, most of the time, basic research is done by the more inexperienced lawyers in the firm, which can take longer and cost you more money and doesn't always result in a great legal product. It's reasonable to ask not to be charged for the basic research that a lawyer who handles your kind of case should already know.

**Preparing Documents.** Most legal work requires drafting documents. They are usually drafted with the help of associates, legal assistants and paralegals and then reviewed by the responsible lawyer.

In the case of more unique documents like motions, legal opinions, and letters, the lawyer will usually dictate the first draft and then review and sign the final document before sending it. Unique documents—those for a specific client and specific need—can require hours of research and drafting to complete. More run-of-the-mill documents can often be generated from a template and shouldn't cost you as much. One reason you should always ask for a bill that identifies the work being done is so you have an idea how much time is being spent on research and drafting of documents.

One issue I've encountered on several occasions is a lawyer preparing a court document using the wrong names. This is usually a sign that a lawyer or his assistant have used a previously drafted document as a template and just added some new information for the new case. This kind of mistake can be very embarrassing for the lawyer, especially if he charged the client as if he'd written a new document.

Lawyers who charge by the hour do not have the right to charge for the time they would have spent if they had to start over from the beginning on every case. You hired your lawyer because he has experience and you agreed to a fair hourly rate that recognized that experience; so you should only have to pay for the time he actually spends working.

**Court Proceedings.** In many cases your lawyer will have to appear in court for hearings and discussions with the judge. This is different from an actual trial in that the lawyer is only going for a short period of time and for a limited purpose.

There will be several status conferences with the judge to set dates and get decisions on disputes between the parties in the case. In civil cases, clients hardly ever attend these proceedings unless the judge specifically requests that one or both of the parties be there.

The biggest frustration that lawyers, and the clients paying for their time, often have is that the proceedings usually require a lot of time for very little actual work done. Lawyers can spend half a day in the court room waiting for the judge to talk to them for 15 minutes. Many times lawyers can group several cases together so you don't end up paying for the whole time they are there. Other times it makes sense to send the most junior lawyer in the firm to attend these hearings, especially if the purpose is to set dates for the case or to argue a motion where the outcome is not really in doubt.

Criminal cases have two important court proceedings that both the lawyer and the client attend: preliminary hearings and procedural hearings. Make sure you're there when your lawyer asks you to be there.

**Discovery Events.** Many kinds of legal cases can require your participation in activities to prepare the case or learn facts. These activities range from interviews, inspections, and phone calls to the more formal depositions and document production.

Depositions are the formal interviews of a party or witness taken under oath. These interviews are almost always recorded and are often videotaped. They can be intimidating if the witness isn't prepared for the intense questioning. The purpose of a deposition is to determine what the people in a case will say and in some cases to try and figure out what happened.

Other discovery events or activities you may be involved in include answering questions submitted by the other side in writing or producing documents requested by another party in the case. The purpose of discovery in a civil case is for both sides to "discover" the facts and what the opposing side is going to say and do in trial.

**Trials.** A trial is a significant event in any case. This is the part of the legal process that most of us see on television, but it is a rare event in real life. Trials take huge amounts of time and resources. In civil cases, the expense of the actual trial can be almost as much as the cost of preparing for the trial.

The truth is, lawyers spend very little of their time in a courtroom. Why? Most cases (more than 95% of civil cases) are resolved by the parties before going to trial. This is due to not only the high cost, but also the lack of control when an uninformed jury makes the final decision.

More criminal cases end up going to trial compared to civil cases because criminal defendants have more at stake, and they hope for a better verdict than they have been offered by the prosecutor.

Trials can be as short as one day or as long as six months for complicated cases with many witnesses. Trials are usually conducted all day, but in some cases a court may have other obligations and the trial will be held only for a portion of each day. Sometimes the parties may decide that they don't want a jury, or in some cases a party isn't entitled to a jury trial and the judge will hear evidence, act as the jury and decide the whole case. This usually results in a quicker trial.

**Appellate Work.** After a case has gone to trial and a verdict has been reached, at least one party in the litigation is going to think that the jury or the judge was wrong. They have the right to appeal the verdicts or decisions of a jury or a judge. Some lawyers specialize in handling this appeal process, writing lengthy legal arguments called *briefs,* and attending the appeal hearing. They argue for their clients and answer questions from the appellate judges, whose job it is to decide if an error has occurred in the underlying trial.

**Lobbying.** Another task that lawyers often engage in is lobbying on behalf of a client to get a law passed or changed. Lobbying is when a lawyer represents a client in trying to persuade a government to change something. This can occur at the city, county, state or the federal level of government. A lawyer representing clients in lobbying has to do extensive research to be effective, and then spend time trying to persuade decision makers to take specific positions. This type of work can be as simple as trying to get zoning laws changed for a piece of property or as complex as getting national laws passed on behalf of an industry.

Many lawyers get involved in local issues that impact the type of legal work they do. But lawyers who represent national clients and try to influence federal policy makers are more likely to specialize in lobbying efforts and develop special expertise and influence.

**Marketing.** Like any business with a service or product to sell, lawyers need to market their services and attract new clients. Lawyers don't usually participate in marketing every day, but they can be involved with arranging advertising, participating in legal organizations that refer clients, meeting with prospective clients, serving in local organizations, and giving presentations for local groups or organizations. The primary focus of most lawyers' legal marketing is to let potential clients know who they are and what type of legal services they offer.

**Administration.** In addition to normal activities related to representing clients, lawyers also have businesses to run. They have to make sure that bills are paid, staff is hired and managed, new lawyers are trained, and that the law firm is operating smoothly. Like any other business, law firms run into business problems that can require extra time to handle. Many firms hire office managers to take care of most of the administration responsibilities, but oversight is always required.

**Miscellaneous.** Lawyers spend time on other regular activities, including continuing education, membership in professional organizations and donated legal work. To maintain their legal licenses lawyers must take classes in new developments in the law, as well as taking regular ethics training. Many lawyers belong to and often take on responsibilities in professional organizations. In addition, many perform free legal work through organizations designed to help provide legal services to those who can't afford them.

## 7.2   Leave It to the Professional

You can help your lawyer to be more effective: stay in communication, cooperate by providing information, and be available for meetings and proceedings.

But some actions and decisions have to be the lawyer's. Three primary areas are driven by the lawyer, and for which you retain the lawyer: (1) deciding the legal strategy, (2) handling the procedure of a case, and (3) developing legal opinions.

**Legal Strategy.** When you hire a lawyer, you usually have a specific legal problem. Whether it's a dispute with someone else or you need specific legal advice or a legal product, you are the customer, and your job is to define the result you're looking for. It's the lawyer's responsibility to determine the best way to get you that result.

Seeking a legal outcome is like guiding an expedition more than it is like building a product. You hire a lawyer with experience guiding travelers on similar journeys and with the understanding that no two trips are the same. Every legal case is unique. An experienced lawyer is your guide to understanding the process, giving advice on the possible outcomes and helping you choose the best way to work toward those outcomes.

**Procedure.** One of the most important things a good lawyer does is handle the complicated process of using the judicial system. Operating in the courts requires practice and tools that good lawyers develop. Experience is important to ensure that deadlines are met and requirements are followed.

This does not mean that people who aren't lawyers can't understand how the system works, but a lot of time is required to learn the rules, and those rules change frequently. Another important part of the legal process is knowing the people who are part of the system: the judges, clerks, administrative staff and other lawyers.

**Legal Opinions.** A legal opinion is an evaluation of how the law applies to your facts. A good and accurate legal opinion is what makes a lawyer and his firm the most valuable to clients. Lawyers know the changing laws in their area of practice and great lawyers have been involved in cases that have made new law or changed existing law.

Working in a specific area of law allows a lawyer to focus on your legal issues and applying the law for your benefit. The advent of case databases have made court decisions readily available to anyone, but the ability to identify why one case applies to your problem and another does not is a valuable skill that takes years for lawyers to develop.

## 7.3  How to Help Your Lawyer

Chapter 8 goes into detail on your responsibilities as a client. This one is more about how you can help your lawyer do his job.

There are two primary areas where you can help your lawyer.

**Be Responsive.** Few things are more frustrating for a lawyer than a client who has high expectations but has no desire to be involved. Trust your lawyer. When he needs information or specific help, go out your way to provide it. Be on time for meetings, provide documents that are required for the case to move forward, and always be honest with your lawyer.

**Do not Perform Legal Work.** This is not an absolute rule. Clients who try to handle some aspects of the case without help, who talk to the other side or opposing lawyer without consulting their own lawyer, perform legal research and "find the answer," or who talk to Uncle Jake (who always wanted to go to law school) about strategy usually create mistrust and frustration. And they cost themselves more money.

If you have extensive experience with your legal issues or have been working with the same lawyer for a long period, you'll develop an understanding of each other's expectations. As the client, you pick the direction, but your matter will be better handled if you leave the driving to a good lawyer.

## 7.4 Malpractice

Here is a secret that some lawyers don't want you to know: they make mistakes. Sometimes lawyers miss deadlines, file the wrong papers, don't prepare well enough, or don't do the right research. Most lawyers are good at what they do, and some are really good. But every so often, even great lawyers make mistakes. When that happens, it's called *malpractice.*

Legal malpractice is when a lawyer fails to perform legal work in a way that a normal lawyer would or should have performed the same work.

This is a very broad standard, because it encompasses not just the work of good lawyers in a specific field, but the mediocre ones as well. If a lawyer commits malpractice you have possible remedies that you can pursue. However, clients can't sue for not getting the result they wanted. You can sue a lawyer for a mistake; you cannot sue because of a bad result.

A clear example of malpractice would be a failure on the part of the lawyer to file an essential document within a time limit. One of the most basic for civil cases is the statute of limitations, or the time you have to pursue a lawsuit against someone else. All states have laws that give statutes of limitations for various actions.

If you've been injured in an auto accident you might hire a lawyer to pursue a claim against the responsible driver. After your lawyer agrees to take the case, he'll collect medical records and accident reports. Malpractice could occur if because of a clerical or calendaring error he misses the deadline for filing your lawsuit.

Because of that error you can no longer file your lawsuit and the responsible driver will refuse to negotiate. Since a normal lawyer is expected to file new lawsuits within the time limits, your lawyer has committed malpractice. In this case you have the right to sue your lawyer. See Chapter 12 for the elements of a successful claim against a lawyer.

Now, let's assume your lawyer files the lawsuit on time, builds your case, the case goes to trial and the jury decides that you're the one responsible for the accident. This is a bad result but as long as your lawyer did everything a normal lawyer should do he didn't commit malpractice and you won't win a malpractice lawsuit.

Many clients are frustrated with their results at the end of the case. In fact, with cases where a jury or judge decide the outcome half of the clients involved are unhappy with the result—there is always a loser!

This is why you need to accept responsibility for the final result of the case and make the important decisions. When the jury comes back with a verdict for the other side it's too late to get another lawyer or negotiate another solution.

# 8. Your Responsibility

*"Lawyers on opposite sides of a case are like the two parts of shears; they cut what comes between them, but not each other."*
*Daniel Webster*

## 8.1 Decisions

**The Final Outcome.** You must make decisions about the direction and final outcome of your case. The legal system can be confusing and frustrating, and your lawyer is your guide and advocate; but you alone can determine when the case is over. You may make the decision to continue to try to "win", pursuing every possible remedy or appeal. Or you may decide to settle or compromise on a resolution. You are the one who makes these decisions and you have to live with the consequences.

In most civil cases, the purpose of litigation is to resolve a dispute. Unless you're retaining a lawyer to do estate planning or to draft legal documents, another party will likely be involved—the opposition.

The opposition wants a different result than you do and within the framework of the law both sides try to obtain their vision of justice. The problem with abandoning your decision-making responsibility is that many lawyers are willing to fight to the end or until your money runs out. The client needs to listen to the counsel of his lawyer and then make the hard decisions.

In criminal cases, fewer decisions need to be made by the client but they they'll likely be more important decisions. In the few criminal cases I've been involved in, a common complaint by the convicted client has been that they didn't understand the decisions that were made and that they felt their lawyer made decisions without their participation. It should always be the client's decision on whether to agree to plead guilty to a crime, negotiate a lesser conviction or take the chance of trying the criminal case in front of a jury.

Lawyers bring their biases, feelings, and personal interests into every case—just like you do. These factors will influence a lawyer's decisions on how to negotiate or resolve a case.

**Limitations.** A client has some responsibility to understand the limitations of the legal system. No legal solution is perfect, and lawyers are not usually any better than you are at predicting the future. Two major limitations of the legal system are that (1) most civil legal problems are solved with money, and (2) neither the court nor the jury will ever see things exactly the way you do.

While big verdicts or unusual legal outcomes attract media attention, most cases are resolved without headlines or news broadcasts. For every story you read about a multi-million dollar verdict thousands of other cases are resolved, tried, won, or lost without huge verdicts.

Most conflicts that become legal problems are settled through negotiation and compromise. It's easier for a lawyer to work with a client who understands that jury trials are risky. Not everyone on a jury will agree with one side or the other and it's unlikely clients will get everything they want simply because they think the law is on their side.

**Hired Gun.** The responsible client doesn't use a lawyer as a weapon. A lawyer has a duty to work within the ethical rules imposed by the state bar. Most lawyers don't enjoy being a hired gun whose purpose is to make the other side suffer.

Most lawyers try not to get as angry or upset as their clients. They can't afford to; they'll continue to work in the same court with the same judges and the same lawyers long after your case is over. Some lawyers do become emotionally involved in their case and are willing to do whatever it takes to win, but these are not usually the most effective lawyers.

A good lawyer is your advocate but will become less effective if his passion becomes so fanatical that he can't give you good counsel.

## 8.2   Be Aware

In many cases a lawyer will work for months or years with minimal interaction with his client, only to discover that the client is unhappy with the end result. The key to not being surprised at the end is for the client to be aware of what's going on while the case is progressing.

**Stay Involved.** Set regular times to discuss what's happening. Make sure to review the documents you receive so that when you talk with your lawyer, you're prepared to ask questions. Insist on regular updates from your lawyer. E-mail can be very useful for this and is a quick way for your lawyer to report on recent events and challenges.

Whatever you do, don't let months pass until your case is almost over and you get a call from your lawyer asking whether you're ready to make important decisions. Only when you stay involved, pay attention, and ask good questions throughout will you be ready when time comes to make important strategic decisions.

**Be Responsive.** Most deadlines in a case are set by the law or by the judge, so when your lawyer asks you to provide information or documents by a certain date take the request seriously. Return telephone calls, answer questions, show up for appointments and follow through on assignments. Failure to respond will not only cost you extra, but could also limit your lawyer's ability to represent you.

**Be Willing to Ask for Information.** Every case is different, and unless you're a lawyer, there will be language and procedures you simply don't understand. Never be afraid to ask the questions. Don't let your lawyer make you feel stupid for asking them. Remember, most lawyers like answering questions, especially if they are getting paid by the hour.

## 8.3   Document Communication

One thing lawyers learn quickly is to always document everything they do, including agreements or understandings with opposing counsel. When dealing with lawyers, follow their example and make sure that every time you have a significant discussion or reach some agreement with your lawyer the communication is documented *in writing*.

You don't have to do it with long letters; emails are a great way to summarize your understanding of conversations or agreements. Of course, some communications, like a fee arrangement, should be in a more formal format like a letter.

So which discussions are significant? Here's a list of some of the events and agreements you should make sure are reduced to writing.

- **Retention agreements.** The scope of the work and the limits on the legal work to be done should be clearly set out.
- **The fee agreement.** This defines how you'll pay for the work and costs that are your responsibility. It also specifies when you'll

receive bills as well as any special arrangements that you negotiate, like who will handle certain kinds of expenses or whether part of the fees will be paid at the end of the case.

- **Action-based discussions.** Record any discussion where decisions are made regarding strategy, resolution, or any action that will require unexpected expenses for you.

- **Decisions and authority.** Any agreement or authority that you gave your lawyer to resolve all or part of your dispute.

- **Status reports.** You may request reports from your lawyer on where the case is and what is going to happen in the future. Keep in mind that status reports cost money, but they're excellent tools to help you understand what the case is about and what options are available. See Chapter 16 for an example outline of a status report.

- **Your Lawyer's Requests.** Any time you're asked for information, documents, or an appearance at a part of the process, confirm what you've been asked to do in writing. This way you can make sure you understand what's being asked and your lawyer can clarify if there's been a misunderstanding.

When you write a letter or e-mail, always include the case number or the name of the case as assigned by the lawyer to identify the file so that your communication will get to the right place.

Writing an e-mail after every telephone call may seem a little extreme, but it takes only minutes, will clarify your understanding and expectations, and will ensure that your lawyer knows what you understood and expect. When you follow up in writing it helps your lawyer stay focused on your case and what you're trying to achieve.

Lastly, *always* keep copies of the documents you create. See Chapter 11 for information on how to organize the documents you receive.

## 8.4   Be Organized

To meaningfully participate in your representation you need to be organized. Legal disputes generate a lot of paper and you'll quickly become intimidated if you don't develop a system for keeping track of the documents you receive and what's happening.

Chapter 11 is about getting organized and gives suggestions for handling the documents you'll receive in a legal case. But here are some suggestions that will help.

| Lawyer-Client Rule Number 7 |
|---|
| Stay organized. You'll receive many documents throughout a case. If you allow them to get unorganized it will be difficult to get organized later and you won't be as informed as you need to be. |

**Keep Everything.** In an average case, you could receive hundreds of pages of documents, and you'll generate more if you print out the e-mails between you and your lawyer. Keep all of these documents. They're the record of your case. You may be surprised which documents become important later on.

**Keep It Safe.** When you start collecting documents and legal papers, find a place where they can be organized and secure. They should be kept out of the way—perhaps even locked up if they contain personal information. Consider common perils such as water or fire damage. By keeping all of your documents in one place you can also ensure that they're disposed of properly at the end of the case. Don't throw confidential documents away; make sure they're *destroyed* when the case has resolved.

**Have a Working File.** A working file is a collection of the important documents that help you, inform you or are originals of agreements or contracts. A good working file is a great resource for getting up to speed before a meeting and for being able to find the documents you use on a regular basis.

**Organize Consistently.** When you receive a letter, report or pleading file it quickly. Too many clients have a case pile or a box in a corner where the documents and letters they receive stack up. When the pile gets big, the task of organizing becomes overwhelming and is often put off. Then it just becomes worse. File things as you receive them and staying organized will be much easier.

## 8.5   Make the Tough Decisions

**The Resolution.** The toughest decision you'll make is how and when to resolve your legal dispute. At some point in most cases the parties either agree to, or are ordered to, participate in a meeting to try to resolve the dispute.

The decision to settle a case or keep going is yours—only yours. Your lawyer will give you advice. He'll make you aware of the consequences of settling or continuing your case. He'll probably be very persuasive on what he thinks should be done, but the final decision is yours.

> **Lawyer-Client Rule Number 8**
> The lawyer advises and advocates. The client decides.

When you are a party in a legal case, you are the one who has to live with the final result. Your lawyer will go on to have many more similar cases. The court will have a never-ending line of cases to process and handle. The opposing lawyer will have more cases as well.

But you and the opposing party will only have *this* case, *this* opportunity to get your dispute resolved. Make sure you understand the consequences as explained by your lawyer. Then make sure that you can live with the consequences of your decisions.

**Settlement.** Most cases are resolved by some sort of a negotiated settlement. A settlement in a legal dispute is usually as formal as the rest of the process. The settlement will be in writing, and sometimes the judge must approve it. The settlement is negotiated between the parties through their lawyers. In some cases, a person called a mediator is brought in to help the parties work through the issues and help the lawyers negotiate.

A negotiated settlement offers you the advantage of some control over the resolution and final outcome. In a negotiation you'll never get everything you want, since the other side has to get something in order for both sides to agree. But you eliminate the risk of a jury deciding to give everything to the other side and nothing to you. Of course, you'll also be giving up the chance for a jury to give you everything you're hoping for.

When lawyers evaluate cases, they'll usually guess their chances of winning by calculating the upside of winning and the downside of losing. I've never seen a case with a 100% chance of winning. In personal injury cases both sides evaluate the chance of winning or losing based on the facts of the case and how the judge will probably allow evidence to be presented.

When I evaluate a case, I guess how many times a reasonable jury would find for my client or my side if I could try the case ten times. I start with the understanding that no matter how *good* a case is, I will always lose it at least one time in ten, and that no matter how *bad* a case is, I'll win it at least once. This is because there are always things that come up in trial that you can't anticipate, and juries who make decisions that make no sense.

If a case can't be settled it usually goes to trial. In trial, anything can happen. You can lose. You may win. But when the jury leaves the courtroom, you cannot control what they decide. You can always settle a case right up to the moment the jury returns with a judgment—you can settle after the verdict, it just may be much harder.

Let's look at how a settlement might work in real life. Take a typical contract dispute where the two sides in litigation are businesses who believe that a contract favors their position. Company A sues Company B, wanting $100,000 in fees for services that were performed. Company B believes that no money is owed. Both sides of this dispute, with the help of their lawyers, evaluate their risks and exposure.

Company A did the work, but has to admit that the contract should have been clearer on whether they should have been paid more. The owners of Company A have to be concerned that if there is a public decision, other clients using the same contract may decide they don't have to pay for the same kinds of services.

Meanwhile, Company B knows that they received the work and knows that the original price of the contract didn't cover the additional expenses in dispute. Both sides evaluate their chances of winning or losing, as well as the additional costs of not resolving the case.

In the end, representatives for the companies meet with the mediator who works out an agreement involving some payment and maybe even an agreement on future services that may be provided under the same agreement.

In the vast majority of legal disputes, the parties finally negotiate and settle their disputes before ever getting to a jury. This is true in all kinds of cases: personal injury, divorces, employment and discrimination cases—even criminal cases, where a settlement is called a *plea bargain*. Resolutions are reached through negotiation and finally a settlement, where both sides give a little so that they can control the outcome.

Because most cases are resolved through settlement, many lawyers who claim expertise as trial lawyers rarely *go* to trial—all of their cases get settled.

Sometimes a client will discover that the closer they get to a real trial, the worse their case gets according to their lawyer. A good reason for getting everything in writing is that you can use these documents in subsequent discussions with your lawyer; who collected fees getting ready for trial and who now claims that you're sure to lose.

**Your Lawyer.** One of the toughest decisions you'll ever make in a legal case is whether you need to find another lawyer. Switching lawyers will cost money. But sometimes it's the right decision. And it's one only you can make.

Frustration with a lawyer is not enough of a reason to fire one. It's almost impossible to deal with a busy professional in a high-stress setting like a legal dispute without feeling some frustration.

Legitimate reasons for deciding to look for another lawyer to handle your case include the following situations.

**Fraudulent Billing.** If you catch your lawyer cheating on his bills, you should probably find another lawyer. Billing you for work that wasn't done, substantial over-billing for easy tasks, or regular "accounting" errors may all be signs of a lawyer you can't trust and someone who isn't concerned about your welfare.

**Lack of Communication.** A failure to call every week shouldn't be a reason to look for a new lawyer. The kind of communication failure you should be concerned about is when you haven't heard from your lawyer in a couple of months and he won't return e-mails or telephone calls.

Unless your lawyer told you that your case won't progress very fast, you should receive some form of communication on a monthly basis—if nothing else, your monthly bill.

You might hire a great lawyer who has the specific skill you are looking for but who is lousy at reporting. In this case, see if someone else in the firm can take responsibility for updates and answering your questions. A consistent lack of communication may be a sign that you need to find another lawyer.

**Lack of Ability.** You may begin to suspect that your lawyer doesn't have the skills you were hoping for. If your lawyer has problems answering your basic questions or doesn't appear comfortable in the courtroom or in the legal proceedings you attend, you need to decide whether you're comfortable with his skill level and knowledge.

Unfortunately, most of the time you *won't* be able to tell if your lawyer is good at what he does. Lawyers usually don't lack for confidence and a few are better at talking the game then playing it. You can rely on your own intuition to make this decision or you can find another lawyer to give you an opinion. Paying another lawyer to review your case will add more expense, but if it's important and you have serious concerns about your lawyer protect yourself and get advice.

**A Lawyer Who Won't Listen.** It's a frustrating problem in dealing with any professional—your lawyer simply doesn't listen. This can create problems when you are trying to explain your objectives and your lawyer is going in a different direction. What typically happens is that you hire a lawyer to handle your problem—a divorce case, for instance—and he has a system in place that includes harassing discovery and scorched-earth legal techniques when what you want is a low-key, non-adversarial and quick resolution of the dispute. If your lawyer won't listen find one who will.

**Personal Issues.** This doesn't refer to the personality conflicts that arise in any relationship, but instead to the personal issues that can impact a lawyer's ability to represent you.

Two important issues that many lawyers deal with are substance abuse and burnout. Lawyers have one of the highest rates of alcohol and substance abuse of the licensed professions. This doesn't mean that most lawyers have this problem, but a lawyer who does can negatively impact your result.

Closely related to substance abuse is burnout. Lawyers work long hours building a practice, and practicing law alone can create stress. Lawyers who are burned out will fail to give you the attention and energy you need.

The signs of a lawyer who may be burned out or have some other personal issue: lack of communication, lack of ability, billing problems, and inability or unwillingness to listen. In addition, lawyers who show passive-aggressive tendencies, lack focus, or exhibit signs of depression may also have issues that need to be resolved before you want them to handle your case.

**Intimate Relationships.** One of the most difficult issues that can arise in a professional relationship is when it becomes inappropriately personal or physical. Lawyers should never date or have intimate relationships with active clients. It's almost impossible for a lawyer to stay objective about a client when the relationship becomes personal. This type of relationship is even more complicated when it involves infidelity with one client from a group of clients.

If you begin a personal relationship with a lawyer you must end the professional one and find another lawyer. Relationships between lawyer and client rarely last and usually cause huge problems. If you're interested in a personal relationship wait until the case is over. Only then approach your lawyer as a person, not your lawyer—and demand that your lawyer do the same until then.

This is your problem. The outcome will impact you and can change your life. You have the ultimate responsibility to make sure you have the right lawyer and that you make the tough decisions.

# 9. Civil Litigation

*"A lawyer is someone willing to spend every cent you have to prove he's right."*

## 9.1 Civil Courts

Civil litigation involves disputes between people and organizations. This section is a very brief and general summary of civil litigation. You need to understand that every state has different ways and laws that govern how civil litigation is handled.

When private citizens have a dispute or need a legal decision that doesn't involve the government, they file their legal case in a civil court. If you sue someone for personal injury, to resolve a contract dispute, or to stop someone from doing something like trespassing on your property, you'll hire a lawyer to file a lawsuit in civil court. There the judge will apply common law or, if applicable, state or federal statutes to resolve your case.

**Common Law**: Law created over time by judges. Most contract law began as common law, developed by judges as they resolved legal cases.

**Statutory Law**: Law created by a statute, or law passed by the legislature of a state or by the Federal Government. For example, bankruptcy law was created by federal law and is administered by special courts—bankruptcy courts—established by the law.

Not all cases will be heard in a regular court. Bankruptcy cases, for example, are governed by federal bankruptcy statutes that also establish special federal courts specializing in bankruptcy matters.

In some states and cities, special family courts are established to deal with divorce, custody, and child-welfare issues. These courts are still considered civil courts, because they don't involve the government prosecuting someone for criminal conduct. Specialty federal courts include:

**U.S. Court of Federal Claims**: A special court where citizens can sue the federal government for money damages from breach of contract or patent infringement (where a person believes that the government infringed on a patent). Claims for personal injury against the federal government are filed in normal federal court.

**U.S. Tax Court**: A court set up to handle tax disputes with the federal government.

**Court of Appeals for Veterans' Claims**: A special court set up to handle and resolve disputes on claims for Veterans' benefits.

**U.S. Court of Appeals for the Armed Forces**: For criminal or civil cases resolved within the military's justice system, all appeals of the court decisions go to this special appeals court made up of civilian judges, many of whom are retired military lawyers and judges.

**U.S. Court of International Trade**: A federal court established to resolve disputes involving foreign governments.

While most civil cases are handled in normal courts, there are different levels of courts for different amounts of money at stake. One of the first things to be determined by your lawyer is which court has the authority to handle your case. Once the right court is determined, the case is filed in that court and officially begins. Different states have different courts and different names for their courts.

**Small-Claims Court**: Small-claims courts are designed to handle simple cases with little money at stake. The parties represent themselves, and the amount that can be awarded is usually limited to between $2,500 and $5,000.

**Lower-Level Court**: Most states have a court which has jurisdiction—or power over—cases where damages are less than some number ($25,000 in many states). The parties usually have lawyers. These courts have a variety of names; what one state calls a *circuit court* may actually be lower- or higher-level court (see below).

**Higher-Level Court**: To get jurisdiction in a higher level court, you have to allege that the dispute has a monetary value of more than a certain value. In many states, the amount will be in excess of $25,000. In recent years, some states have raised this threshold because $25,000 isn't as big a sum as it used to be. Other common thresholds are $50,000 or even $100,000.

**Family Courts**: These are usually set up to handle domestic disputes like divorces, child support, and custody issues. In smaller cities or rural areas, there may not be enough cases to justify a special family court.

**Probate Courts**: A state court designed to handle wills and estate matters.

## 9.2 Rules and Procedures

The process of litigation is controlled by rules that have to be followed in every case. These rules are usually called the Rules of Civil Procedure and are similar from state to state. However, every state has its own rules and there are important differences that will significantly affect your case.

The most common differences are the deadlines and procedures for filing cases, but sometimes the rules establish specific requirements important in just one state. Federal court also has its own rules. Many states use the federal rules as a guide, but make their own changes. These rules are authorized by a state's supreme court. In some cases courts in a city or county may add or modify the rules.

If you have a chance to read or review the Rules of Civil Procedure for your state, you'll soon realize that they are confusing and disorganized. For example, the rules about who has a right to a trial are usually found in the trial section, but the rules on beginning a lawsuit are not. Important rules and procedures can be difficult to find if you don't know where to look. Like any legal standards the rules are subject to interpretation by the courts in your state and especially by the judge.

## 9.3 Beginning the Lawsuit

**Pre-Lawsuit Activity.** Before filing a lawsuit, your lawyer will do a lot of work, completing the initial investigation to prepare and evaluate the case. There should be opportunities to seek resolution before a lawsuit is started. Your lawyer will probably contact the other side or their lawyer to see if there can be a settlement or agreement to resolve the issue.

Lawyers can agree to share information, allow interviews, and will exchange letters setting out positions and possible settlements. In many cases, conflicts can be resolved without any litigation at all, but if the dispute cannot be resolved, then a formal lawsuit is started.

**Complaint.** A lawsuit begins when one party files a complaint in the appropriate court with the authority to decide the case. The complaint is a legal document describing the allegations being made, identifying the persons suing and being sued, and stating the relief sought. Relief is the remedy you're asking the court or the jury to give you. Relief can mean money, or it could be a request for some equitable relief, such as returning property or forcing the other party to finish a contract.

The requested relief can be a specific amount, but more often, a plaintiff will simply claim that the damages are an unspecified amount in excess of whatever the minimum is that the court has the authority to award. See the example in 9.4 for a simple complaint from an auto accident.

In some states, the complaint can be very short, not providing much detail about what is claimed by the plaintiff—the person who is suing. Other states require lots of information, and the complaint is like a short story explaining the facts and circumstances that led to the complaint being filed.

Some claims, like complaints that allege fraud, require the allegations and facts to be well-explained. Every complaint also includes the counts—the specific claims—allowed by law. A basic element of a lawsuit is that the plaintiff has a right to sue, so the complaint needs to include the legal basis or the legally recognized claim that supports the reason for the lawsuit.

For example, with breach of contract or fraud a statute usually gives the plaintiff the right to sue. The complaint must refer to this statute or at least be written in the language of the law that supports the right to sue. The last thing the complaint contains is the request or claim for relief, sometimes referred to as the "prayer for relief."

In a complaint, each separate fact and allegation is usually given a separate paragraph, and each paragraph is numbered. This helps the court and opposing lawyers quickly refer to each point of the complaint and provide a response, called the answer.

**The Summons.** Once the complaint has been filed, the court issues a summons, a document informing the person being sued—the defendant—that a lawsuit has been filed, where it has been filed, and when. Once he receives the summons and the complaint, he is said to have been served.

**Service of Process.** This is the formal procedure used to make sure that a defendant receives the lawsuit. Sometimes a process-service professional will deliver the documents to a defendant. Members of a sheriff's department or other law enforcement officers also handle this responsibility and will try to find the defendant at home or at work and deliver the lawsuit and summons.

In some cases, a friend or acquaintance of the plaintiff can serve the lawsuit, but the rules usually require that someone who has no connection to the parties deliver it and sign a statement that the defendant received the summons and complaint.

Once the defendant has received the pleadings and summons he will have a limited amount of time to provide an answer. If he fails to respond within the time limit on the summons, the plaintiff can request that a judgment be given, called a default judgment.

Usually court fees must be paid when you file a complaint. Having the complaint served will also cost money, and this is in addition to the cost of preparing the documents. From the beginning, the lawsuit will cost the plaintiff money.

## 9.4   Pleadings and Motions

Pleadings and motions are the official documents filed throughout the litigation by both sides in the case. Pleadings are the official documents filed, or sent, by the parties in the case. Motions are formal requests asking the judge to take specific action. Both of these types of legal documents must be written in a set format and filed with the court within time limits established by the rules or determined by the judge. There are many kinds of pleadings and motions, but some that are common to all litigation.

**Answer.** When the defendant receives the complaint, the first pleading that he usually files is an answer. The answer is a pleading that provides the defendant's response to the plaintiff's version of the facts, responds to the specific allegations, and sets out possible legal defenses to the allegations. Just like the complaint lists all of the facts in separately numbered paragraphs, the answer follows that same format and gives the defendant's side of the story. The defendant also can dispute the allegations and list defenses. For example, in the dispute below involving an auto accident, the plaintiff alleges that the defendant ran a red light. The allegations and responses may look something like this:

| THE COMPLAINT - Plaintiff: | THE ANSWER - Defendant: |
|---|---|
| 1. Plaintiff had a green light and was hit by the Defendant who ran a red light. | 1. Defendant denies this allegation and claims that he had a green light and the right of way, and it was the Plaintiff who ran the red light. |
| 2. Plaintiff alleges that the Defendant was negligent in running the red light and causing injuries to the Plaintiff. | 2. Defendant denies negligence and alleges that if anyone was negligent it was the Plaintiff. |
| 3. Plaintiff alleges that she was injured as a result of the accident and wants damages in excess of $25,000. | 3. Defendant doesn't know if Plaintiff was really injured, but doubts the injuries are as bad as alleged. |

This is a simplified example. Most complaints and the corresponding answers will go on for pages and pages. The purpose of the initial pleading is to describe the facts and the positions of the two sides so that the legal conflict can be defined.

**Motion for Summary Judgment.** A motion for summary judgment is a pleading that requests the judge issue a verdict before the case is presented to a jury. Because the jury is usually responsible for determining the facts of a case, the judge would grant this motion only if there were no real question of what happened.

In the above example, a summary judgment would be appropriate only if both sides agreed that the light was red for the defendant. This isn't likely to happen, but it could if the defendant isn't disputing that he ran a red light and instead believes that plaintiff is exaggerating his damages. The plaintiff can file a motion for summary judgment and point out that the defendant admitted running the light. The judge can agree that on the issue of the red light there is no dispute and grant the motion, at least for the question of negligence.

Either side can file this type of motion during the case, but unless there are no real arguments or disputed facts regarding what happened, summary motions are rarely granted.

**Counter-Claim.** A counter-claim is a set of claims and a request for relief by a defendant against a plaintiff. When a defendant files or makes a counter-claim, the plaintiff has to file an answer just as if she had been sued first.

In the example above, if the defendant believes that it was the plaintiff who actually ran the red light, he can sue for his own damages. This claim or countersuit can be included as part of the answer, or it can be filed later as a separate pleading.

**Cross-Claim.** A cross-claim is when a defendant believes that another defendant in the case is either entirely responsible or caused the plaintiff damages as well.

Let's say that there were actually three cars involved in this accident. The plaintiff has sued the two other drivers because both of them ran the red light. One of the drivers may file a cross-claim if he was hit from behind and pushed into the intersection. In that case he may file a claim as part of his defense *and* for his own damages.

**Third-Party Complaint.** A third-party claim is a pleading that accuses a person not named in the lawsuit of being responsible for what happened. In this case, the defendant might bring a third-party claim if he believes, or has evidence, that both drivers had a green light because the light was malfunctioning. In this case, he can argue that he had the right of way and that it is the city or manufacturer of the light who's responsible for the accident and the damages.

**Amended Complaint.** As the lawsuit continues, the facts and theories of the case may change. In our story above, once everyone knows who the witnesses are and what they have to say and the light has been inspected the plaintiff may realize the scope of the lawsuit has changed and will file an amended complaint.

An amended complaint is similar to the first complaint but changes are made to the facts, claims or to the claimed damages. If the plaintiff files an amended complaint the defendant will then file an amended answer that deals with the new allegations or claims.

**Motions.** Throughout the litigation, the various lawyers will file many motions. Motions have to follow a specific format and pattern, but the motions filed are as varied as the types of cases that are brought. These motions generally fall into three categories.

*Motions to Resolve Disputes.* Lawyers on the opposite sides of cases don't always see eye to eye. When they disagree one side can file a motion with the judge asking him to resolve the dispute. Examples of these kinds of motions include motions to compel—force—the other side to do something, motions to respond to a pleading, to allow access to documents or property, or to get cooperation with the court's schedule. Another type of motion to resolve a dispute would be one seeking help from what one side considers abusive process.

Abusive process may occur when one side tries to request documents or personal information that has nothing to do with the lawsuit, then the lawyer may ask the judge to strike, or quash, the request.

*Motions regarding the time limits and schedule in the case.* In most states, when a lawsuit is filed and answered the judge has a meeting with the lawyers where they create a schedule of discovery dates, and in some cases actually set the trial date. These initial dates are rarely followed but lawyers usually have to get the judge's permission to change them. Sometimes disputes arise about the schedule and who goes first in producing information or witnesses. In these cases the motion is a combination of solving a dispute and scheduling dates for the lawsuit.

*Motions seeking some relief (help) or a decision.* These motions seek a decision from the judge about the merit of one side of the case. An example would be a motion for summary judgment where one side asks the judge to decide the case instead of waiting for the trial when it's evident that one side should win because of the law or strength of facts.

In our example, if the plaintiff can produce multiple witnesses or a video of the accident and the defendant can't find anyone to support his story, the judge may determine that the law requires the plaintiff to win because there's no evidence to support the defendant. But if the witnesses aren't sure, there's no video and the drivers have conflicting stories, then a jury gets to decide what really happened and the judge won't grant the motion.

Parties sometimes seek relief or assistance from the judge while the lawsuit is still going on. If property is involved, one party may ask the court to make sure that it's taken care of. A party can ask the judge for a restraining order if there's a chance of physical harm from the other party. These types of relief are usually temporary, but can be made permanent if a party requests permanent relief and if the law gives the judge the power to do it.

## 9.5 Parties

The people or organizations that participate in a lawsuit are called the parties in, or to, the lawsuit. The plaintiff starts the lawsuit, and the defendant is the person being sued. These are the parties.

The section of the rules on parties deals with the issue of who can sue and be sued. Most states require that the parties to a case be the age of majority—usually 18—and be capable of participating in the decisions in the litigation. If defendants are not capable of participating meaningfully but have valid claims, courts can appoint someone to represent them.

For the purpose of a lawsuit a business or corporation is treated as a person in terms of the right to sue or be sued and in the application of the rules, although a business can't represent itself and has to hire a lawyer.

Three different kinds of special lawsuits for special circumstances are identified and explained in this section that describes parties to litigation and their rights.

**Interpleader.** The purpose of an interpleader is to distribute property or assets that multiple people claim. Rather than fight all of them, the person or organization that is the defendant gives the assets to the court, puts everyone on notice that the judge is going to split up the assets and then walks away.

A classic interpleader is a situation where a bank holds a bank account with money claimed by several people. The bank doesn't want to be sued by all of them so the bank files an interpleader lawsuit, gives the money to the court and then lets the people who claim it fight and split it up.

**Class Action.** This is a lawsuit where many people have similar claims against one defendant or a small group of defendants. Class actions are usually very lucrative for the lawyers; lawyers who file class-action lawsuits usually specialize in this type of litigation. These lawsuits require common facts, common claims, and similar injuries. Usually several plaintiffs called class plaintiffs represent the class as a whole, and their claims are representative of the proposed group. When a class-action is filed, the judge reviews the nature of the shared claims and decides whether to certify, or approve, the class. Class-actions allow a large group of plaintiffs to take advantage of a single trial of the common facts.

For example, let's say that a manufacturer is accused of making a defective product that has injured many people. In a traditional legal system every plaintiff would have to prove that the manufacturer was negligent and in some cases, the plaintiff might win, but in other cases, with different jurors, the manufacturer might win.

This result wouldn't be fair, since juries have already decided the defendant's negligence. To avoid this problem, the courts devised a system where a group of plaintiffs, the class representatives, can bring a lawsuit on behalf of all people who suffered the same kind of injury. If the case goes to trial, the basic issues are decided by a single jury. In this example, the jury decides whether or not the manufacturer was negligent. So class-action suits are winner-take-all litigation.

Defendants fight the use of the class action as vigorously as they can because they have so much to lose. Losing a class action can be devastating for a defendant since every plaintiff now can claim that the basic facts have been decided. The only remaining issue would be the amount of the damages, and this is resolved by a settlement or a much shorter trial for each plaintiff who claims he has been injured.

The downside for plaintiffs is that if the defendant wins every plaintiff is out of luck and all of the cases relating to the alleged negligence are over. When a class action goes to trial both sides pull out all the stops because so much is at stake. Few class actions go to trial; when the judge approves a class the sides usually try to settle the case. The class representatives and the lawyers usually get great settlements but the individuals who are bound by the settlement may not make out as well.

**Derivative Actions by Shareholders.** Several other categories of parties are identified by the rules but the only other action for a specific party that you may hear of is a derivative action by shareholders. This action allows a shareholder in a public company to sue the company. This is complicated litigation. The problem with suing a company you own stock in is that as a stockholder you're an owner—so you're really suing yourself. Like class actions the lawyers who represent shareholders usually specialize in this litigation.

## 9.6 Depositions and Discovery

Most of the lawyer's time spent on a case in litigation is actually spent in preparation or discovery. This term describes everything the lawyer does to find out the facts, define the issues and try to learn how each side is going to prove their case.

Discovery is the most frustrating time for a client. It can take years to get a case ready with little activity and lots of legal bills. To conduct discovery, lawyers send and request documents. Both sides take depositions of possible witnesses. The purpose of these activities is for both sides to make sure that they won't be surprised by facts or testimony in the trial. Discovery also lays the groundwork for settlement of the case.

**Duty of Disclosure.** The federal rules require both sides to disclose all the facts they know. The rule generally requires both sides to file a statement of the case that states who they think will be witnesses, and what facts and evidence exist in the case. The purpose is to reduce the expense and time for discovery by requiring both sides to disclose all the facts, both good and bad. The reality is that the rule just gives lawyers something else for lawyers to fight about.

Discovery is a game between the lawyers—each trying to find out what the other side knows and is going to do, while at the same time not giving away information or strategy. Lawyers spend a great deal of time during this phase filing motions and legal documents in an attempt to discover what the other side knows and how they intend to pursue their case.

There are a variety of tools that are used in discovery:

**Interrogatories.** These are written questions sent to the parties. Interrogatories are used to get general information such as the name and addresses of the parties or information about the allegations or defenses. Sometimes the questions will be about the evidence or identifying the people in an organization who might know something about a case. Lawyers carefully draft the answers so they're truthful, but not helpful.

**Requests for Documents.** Lawyers ask for all of the documents related to a case. Requests for both documents and evidence have to be very specific, identifying the nature of the document, the time frame and sometimes where the lawyers or parties think they may be located. Request for documents are as broad as possible and usually include long lists of the different formats that documents might take: such as papers, letters, emails, electronic files, databases . . . the list can go on forever!

**Request for Inspection.** A formal request to look at something or somewhere the other side controls. For example, if you need to inspect a piece of equipment, or if an accident occurred on private land, your lawyer will need to make a formal request to look at the property or have an expert inspect the item or property.

**Depositions.** A formal recorded interview of a witness or a party in a lawsuit where the person testifying has taken an oath to be truthful. The purpose of the deposition is to find out what a person knows and what they'll say if a case goes to trial. Depositions are not only important for what a lawyer can find out, but also for what they can get a person to say because a lawyer is always looking for phrases and answers—sound bites—that can be used later to support the case.

In most depositions a court reporter is present and asks the witness to take an oath to tell the truth. The opposing lawyer then asks questions about the case, about the person, and about anything else that could possibly be important later. Depositions can be videotaped. Sometimes they can be used as evidence in a trial if the person isn't available to testify when the trial starts.

Depositions are one of the biggest expenses in a legal case. Your lawyer will bill for time spent preparing for each deposition, time spent taking the deposition and time spent after the deposition trying to figure out the impact of the person's testimony. When your lawyer proposes taking lots of depositions make sure you understand why he needs the sworn testimony of every person on the list.

On the other hand if the testimony of a person is important to the case don't be cheap. You need to know what that person is going to say and some witness's testimony needs to be preserved so they can't change it later.

In a trial depositions are used in a variety of ways. Because they're given while the witness is under oath they can be used as evidence to support motions filed with the court. Depositions can be used by other witnesses, including experts, to form an opinion about the case. Most important, deposition testimony can be used as testimony in the trial or to question the witness who gave the deposition.

If a witness isn't available for the trial the deposition may be used as a substitute for live testimony. The rules on the use of a deposition vary from state to state but most allow the transcript to be used to present evidence to the court or to the jury. In some cases, depositions are specifically taken to be presented to a jury as the testimony of the witness. These depositions are a little more formal and tend to follow the rules of court more than the typical deposition intended for discovery.

If you're a party in the litigation you can attend depositions. It can be both interesting and helpful to attend depositions of key witnesses in a case. If you attend, follow your lawyer's instructions. Don't allow yourself to become part of—or disrupt—the deposition if you get angry or upset about what's being said.

**Impeachment.** Using evidence to prove—or try to prove—that a witness isn't telling the truth. Depositions are a very useful tool when a witness changes his or her story in trial or when a lawyer believes that a witness may have lied in a deposition. Impeachment occurs when the lawyer is able to show that a witness did not tell the truth in some part of his testimony in trial or earlier in the case.

If the witness has lied the deposition can be used to show what the witness previously said, and in some cases, to question the honesty of the witness generally. Impeachment can also be accomplished with other discovery tools or any evidence showing that a witness isn't telling the truth or has changed his story.

**Physical or Mental Examinations.** In some cases the health or condition of one of the parties is a major issue of the litigation. In such cases the other side can request that the party be seen by a medical doctor or specialist who will act as a witness in the case.

The classic example is a plaintiff who alleges that he's been injured. The defendants can ask the court for permission to have the plaintiff examined by a doctor to determine the extent and long-term impact of the injuries.

These exams are often called Independent Medical Exams or IMEs. If the mental status of a party is at issue the court may allow an examination by a mental health professional. Or, if the person's mental status is a major issue in the case (such as in a competency hearing), the judge can order the examination himself and choose the medical professional who does the exam.

**Requests for Admission.** A request for admission is when one side asks the other side in a written pleading to admit a specific fact that is true. Usually these requests are made about pretty clear issues such as the location of an accident or some fairly well-documented fact. The concept is that if both sides agree then neither side has to prove that point. Sometimes these requests are made to help impeach a party if they fail to admit something you can show they knew to be true.

**Failure to Cooperate in Discovery.** If one side fails to cooperate in providing information appropriately requested the other side can, and usually will, ask the judge to force cooperation. Usually the judge won't decide whether the information is truthful—that's the jury's role. But the judge will get involved if one side fails to respond, provide answers, or share information when it's been requested.

Discovery in litigation is supposed to be done within specific deadlines and time limits. When written questions are submitted the rules give the answerer a specific amount of time to respond. Usually all depositions have to be completed within deadlines as well. The lawyers can sometimes agree on altering deadlines but most times they have to get the judge's permission to make substantial schedule changes.

At times a discovery request is very difficult to respond to or asks for information that has nothing to do with the case. In these instances, the lawyer can ask the judge to decide whether the information needs to be provided, but the lawyer cannot just refuse to respond. In some states a lawyer can file a formal objection to a request and then the burden shifts back to the other side to show why the information is needed. In the end the judge will decide whether the question has to be answered or the information provided.

**Sanctions.** If one side fails to follow the rules of discovery, the court can impose sanctions—punishments that are usually monetary damages for the time spent by the other side to get the information. However the judge has the authority to impose very serious consequences, including deciding that the party that failed to provide information has lost all or part of the case. This type of sanction is devastating so make sure that you are aware of discovery requests and are working with your lawyer to get information and responses submitted on time.

## 9.7 Trials

Every movie or story about a legal battle concludes dramatically with a trial where the lawyers face off and do battle for the hearts and minds of the jury as life-changing decisions are made and justice is done to the satisfaction of all. In reality a trial is slow and boring and at the end only one side believes that justice has been done.

Very few civil cases make it to trial. The statistics vary from state to state, but generally less than five percent of cases filed in civil court end up being decided by a jury. Some cases are dismissed by the judge, some are abandoned by one of the parties, and most are resolved by the parties before trial begins with a compromise agreement or settlement of the claims. A few clients will risk everything for their day (or their weeks) in court.

**The Judge and the Jury.** The purpose of a trial is to decide the facts that are being disputed. The judge's role is to decide who can sue and what rules or laws apply. The judge also decides what evidence the jury gets to hear and what the decisions of the jury mean. The function of the jury is to listen to conflicting evidence and decide which evidence has the most weight or is most likely to be the truth.

**Right to a Jury Trial.** In many civil cases the parties have a right to a jury trial, meaning they cannot be refused a jury if they ask for it. In civil cases the jury will be made up of six to twelve members. More and more states are opting for smaller juries because the traditional jury of twelve people is more expensive and difficult to assemble.

**Trial by Jury or by the Court.** Just because the parties have a right to a jury doesn't mean that they have to use one. If both parties agree the judge can act as a jury, deciding not only the questions of law but also the facts. This is often called a "bench" trial since the trial is played to the bench where the judge sits. The advantages of a trial before a judge include a faster process and a better chance of having a more educated decision, especially when the trial deals with technical facts or questions of law. The advantage of juries is that they can represent the members of a community and are more likely to be swayed by emotional arguments.

Some cases don't have a right to a jury because of a law or when a claim involves an administrative agency of the government. A statute may require you to use a specific court or type of process instead of a jury. Sometimes this is because the type of case requires specialized knowledge that a jury won't have, and sometimes it's simply because lots of claims and lawsuits (as in many worker's compensation statutes and systems) make it too expensive to have a jury for every case.

**Selection of Jurors.** Jurors are selected from a jury pool; a large group of people selected for possible jury duty The lawyers usually participate in picking the jurors who will decide the facts. How much participation the lawyers have is a function of the state rules and the individual judge. Sometimes picking a jury can take weeks because the lawyers are allowed to interview every possible juror for as long as they want. Other states or courts allow only the judge to ask questions of jurors and a jury can be chosen in the morning with the trial beginning after lunch.

The process of questioning and qualifying the jury is called voir dire. This French phrase means, "to speak the truth." Through voir dire the lawyers determine if potential jurors are qualified and not prejudiced against the parties. Jurors are usually asked if they know any of the parties or the lawyers in the case. Sometimes they're asked whether they've been involved in a similar case or have had family or friends who have been parties in a similar case. The goal is to make sure that jurors can be fair.

Jurors can be dismissed for a variety of reasons. Many can't serve because of employment or family obligations. Some aren't qualified or have a bias that one side or the other believes would lead to a flawed decision. An example would be a prospective juror who believes that women are bad drivers and might vote against a woman driver in an accident no matter what the evidence shows. If bias is this clear, the lawyers can ask the judge to dismiss or exclude a person from the jury. As potential jurors are dismissed from a trial they may be allowed to go home or they may have to return to the jury pool to see if they can serve on another jury.

The lawyers can ask for jurors to be removed from a possible jury without giving a reason. This is called a challenge. The number of challenges in a case is limited so lawyers have to be careful when they choose to remove a potential juror. For each person who is rejected, another potential juror is called from the pool. Lawyers usually have only two or three challenges so they hope to get a jury that will be sympathetic to their client. When all of the challenges have been used the jury is chosen.

**Consolidation or Separate Trials.** One of the decisions the judge may have to make is how many trials there should be for a case. If a plaintiff files separate lawsuits against several different defendants for the same event or type of damages the judge may decide that these separate lawsuits are really about the same thing and will consolidate the different lawsuits into one trial. This can happen when a plaintiff alleges that several defendants are responsible for the same injuries. The defendants can ask the judges to consolidate the cases into one trial so there isn't double recovery and so the jury can decide which defendant is responsible.

On the flip side, in some cases a plaintiff may sue multiple defendants as a single case and the defendants may believe that their cases are very different and will ask the judge for separate trials. This can occur when the allegations or damages are completely different for each defendant or when a defendant believes and the judge agrees that having all of the defendants in the same trial could result in injustice.

**Subpoena.** In a trial both sides want to present witnesses. Not all witnesses voluntarily come to trial or even to their depositions, so the rules allow lawyers to issue subpoenas. A subpoena is an order for a witness to appear in court, in a legal proceeding, or for someone to bring a specific item such as business records or a piece of property to a proceeding. A subpoena is an official court petition and anyone who receives one is required to either appear on the date and time given or file a motion with the judge asking for permission to change or stop the request. There are legitimate reasons for a judge to decide that a witness is excused from appearing but make sure you get advice from a lawyer before ignoring a subpoena.

**Opening Statements.** Throughout the trial only a couple of opportunities exist for the lawyers to talk directly to the jury. The most common are opening statements and closing arguments.

Lawyers are limited in their ability to explain what evidence means. One of the important roles of the judge is to limit the argument or explanatory speeches by lawyers. In fact, the only time that a lawyer is supposed to explain what the evidence means or appeal to the jury is closing argument, since the opening statement is supposed to be about the facts.

Opening statements are a summary of the facts of the case. Lawyers are supposed to limit emotional appeals or explanations, and not engage in giving arguments. Arguments are defined as the lawyer trying to explain what the evidence means, drawing conclusions and appealing to the jury to interpret the evidence in a specific way. In the opening statement, lawyers are supposed to simply tell the jury what evidence will be presented in the trail.

In some courts, a lawyer may be able to argue in his opening statement about what the evidence will prove and what verdict the jury should arrive at, but the general purpose of the opening statement is to introduce the parties, explain the case, and outline the evidence to be presented. Many lawyers believe that a good opening statement is essential to winning a case because juries decide early in the case who will win.

**Plaintiff Goes First**. Throughout a trial, the plaintiff usually goes first. The plaintiff's lawyer makes the first opening statement and the defendant follows. The plaintiff presents evidence first, calls witnesses then finishes his case before the defendant starts.

When the defendant finishes presenting evidence, the plaintiff gives closing argument first, followed by the defendant. The plaintiff is allowed to address the jury last in a "rebuttal" closing. The principle is that plaintiff has the burden to prove his case and should have the first chance to present evidence and the last chance to talk to the jury through his lawyer.

**Evidence.** Presenting evidence is the heart of a trial. It is also the least-interesting part, especially when a trial goes on for a long time. Since the jury's job is to decide the facts, the trial is to present all of the known, admissible facts. Often the evidence from the two sides will conflict. The jury must then decide which evidence is most credible and make a decision.

Evidence is presented through exhibits and witnesses.

Exhibits are the tangible physical evidence used to demonstrate the facts of the case. They can range from documents and photos to actual objects like equipment or even models that help illustrate a point.

Witnesses are called—or selected—by the lawyers for both sides. A witness takes an oath to tell the truth and then answers questions from the lawyer. Questions have to be asked in the right way or the other side will object. The rules on how to ask questions are confusing but are designed to ensure that a witness testifies only to things he knows about personally and to things that are of value to the case.

The lawyer who calls the witness asks questions first. The other lawyer is then allowed to cross-examine the witness. Cross-examination can be difficult for witnesses since the objective is to discredit witnesses or their testimony. Since a lawyer wants to prove his client's version of the facts the lawyer's goal is to discredit witnesses called by the other side.

**Cross-Examination.** When a lawyer calls a witness to testify, the opposing lawyer has the right to question—cross-examine—that witness to clarify the testimony or attack what was said. Usually the opposing lawyer will have his own witnesses about the facts, so the purpose of cross-examination is to challenge the credibility of the testimony or the witness.

The type of question used in cross-examination is a leading question. A leading question leads the witness to a specific answer or is asked in such a way that the witness has to answer yes or no without an explanation.

Being a witness in this process can be frustrating, because it can be hard to answer questions about complicated issues with just *yes* or *no*. The key to answering leading questions is to listen carefully, answer as truthfully as possible and, if allowed, ask the judge for permission to elaborate when a short yes or no isn't enough.

There are several types of leading questions:

*Presupposing Questions:* These questions assume facts that might not be true. For example, "Have you quit smoking?" only makes sense if you've smoked at some time. If you've never smoked, you really can't answer this question yes or no.

*"If" Questions:* These questions give hypothetical situations and ask for your response. An "if" question could be, "If the light was red when you entered the intersection, then you'd be responsible for this accident?" The answer to this question is always yes, but the question makes no sense if you know the light was not red and the other party ran the light.

*Context or Perspective Questions:* Many times a leading question tries to reframe the context of a witness' testimony, so they are called context or perspective questions. They try to make an issue out of peripheral issues, such as conditions, ability, or background. In some cases, a witness may have special knowledge—such as an expert—and the purpose of the cross-examination is to try to question the knowledge and bias of the expert.

*Credibility Questions.* Credibility is the issue of how much weight a jury should put on a witness's testimony. Sometimes a lawyer will try to show that a witness has less credibility because of some aspect of his knowledge or an interest in the outcome.

It can be as simple as one eyewitness being further away than another, or a witness having said different things at different times. Credibility may mean that one witness is less reliable than another or that a specific witness isn't reliable at all. Witnesses who appear to be biased can also have their creditability challenged. For example, the credibility of a relative can be challenged if his account is different from the other witnesses'.

**Experts.** A special kind of witness in a trial, an expert may be needed when the average person lacks the knowledge or expertise to determine a fact in the case. Experts are usually people who have education or experience allowing them to testify about something technical or complicated, for example a medical expert testifying about the meaning of a medical test. Since the average person probably wouldn't know how to interpret such a result an expert can educate the jury and explain the facts.

Experts are used in many trials. They explain how machines work or testify about calculating damages. Experts are almost always are involved in cases against professionals such as doctors, accountants and lawyers, since knowing how a professional should have acted requires expertise. Experts can be used to provide valuations of property and they can testify in cases where the mental status of a witness or party is an issue.

The biggest problem with using experts is that both sides use them and their testimony is usually exactly the opposite. The plaintiff's expert will say that the medical tests show a severe injury while the defendant's expert testifies that the tests don't show *any* injury. Experts are also very expensive because they charge for their time.

In recent years a number of reforms have been instituted to fix some of these problems. Judges have more power to disqualify experts who appear to be creating opinions for money. But determining whether an expert is credible can be hard for a judge. Another reform allows judges to appoint experts who will be more neutral to render opinions. The problem with both of these reforms is that it goes against the basic philosophy of allowing parties to present their own case; so most judges allow each side's experts to testify and then instruct the jury to decide which expert was the most believable.

**Objections.** The purpose of a trial is to determine the most likely truth when there are conflicting sides. The truth in question can be as simple as which party ran a red light or as complicated as an international contract dispute. No matter what the issues are, rules guide how evidence is presented, what questions can be asked and how questions can be answered.

Throughout the trial, lawyers listen carefully as the other side asks questions. If a question isn't appropriate an objection is made; the listening lawyer stands up and *objects,* explaining why he didn't like the question. The judge allows the other lawyers to respond and then makes a decision. If the objection is sustained, the question isn't answered and the questioning lawyer will have to find another way to get the desired information or answer. If the objection is overruled the question is allowed and must be answered by the witness.

In some cases a question is asked and answered before the lawyer can make an objection. If either the question or the answer is inappropriate the judge can instruct, or tell the jury to disregard both the question and the answer.

Here is a list of some of the more common objections:

*Ambiguous, Confusing, Misleading, Vague, Unintelligible.* A lawyer can make an objection to a question that is not clearly asked. The witness and the jury need to know what information is being sought and what the answer means.

*Arguing the Case.* Lawyers try to argue their case all through the trial, meaning they try to explain to the jury what the evidence means. When presenting evidence lawyers are only allowed to present the evidence, not argue it. This type of objection might be made in opening statements where lawyers try to argue the case before any evidence is presented or during presentation of evidence when lawyers make statements or speeches instead of asking questions of a witness.

*Arguing the Law.* It is the judge's job to explain the law to the jury. The witnesses are there to present the facts. If a lawyer gets carried away in arguing with a witness or trying to explain the law or how it applies you may hear this objection.

*Argumentative.* An argumentative question is one where the lawyer states a conclusion and then asks the witness to agree with it or dispute it. A question is argumentative when it's really just a speech by the lawyer, and the answer isn't that important, such as, "Since it was raining and you don't see that well and you weren't paying attention you didn't see the red light and you ran it, didn't you?"

*Asked and Answered.* Lawyers will often try to emphasize a point by repeating questions. Limited repetition may be allowed but most judges will sustain this objection if the same question has been asked two or three times.

*Prejudicial or Inflammatory Evidence.* Judges are not supposed to allow evidence that unfairly prejudices or inflames a jury. For example, a lawyer shouldn't ask questions which might create the impression that the defendant has a long history of prior criminal conduct especially if that history has nothing to do with the trial. Questions about the background of a witness might be important depending on the type of case but shouldn't be allowed to influence a jury when it has nothing to do with the trial.

*Assumes Facts not in Evidence.* Lawyers can object when the introduction to a question assumes a fact that has not or cannot be proved.

*Beyond the Scope.* When a lawyer calls a witness to testify the cross-examination by the other side must be limited to the information given by the witness during the direct examination. If lawyers want to ask for new information they must wait until the direct examination of a witness they have called.

*Calls for Speculation.* A question that asks a witness to guess is not appropriate. Witnesses are supposed to testify of what they know from personal experience or expertise. A witness who was first to respond to an accident can testify as to what he did and saw, but it isn't appropriate for the witness to testify as to what probably happened to cause the accident since he didn't actually see it.

*Compound Question.* Two or more separate questions asked at the same time. Asking a witness two yes or no questions at the same time can be confusing since the jury may not be certain which part of which question is being answered.

*Hearsay.* This occurs when a witness tells the jury what someone else said. For example, if a witness to an accident is asked what another witness to the accident said about it this is hearsay. A witness is supposed to testify as to what she personally saw or knows. A judge wants to avoid evidence coming in that can't be evaluated or evidence from witnesses who cannot be cross-examined because they aren't in court.

*Leading.* A leading question tries to influence the answer. "You had a green light when you entered the intersection, didn't you?" The lawyer shouldn't be doing the testifying. Leading questions can be used in cross-examination. In some cases a judge may allow leading questions with witnesses who have trouble testifying or with hostile, evasive, or adverse witnesses.

*Misstating the Evidence or the Law.* A lawyer can make reasonable assumptions about the evidence or about previous testimony but will get an objection if evidence or the law is misstated or misquoted.

*Narrative.* Lawyers are not supposed to ask open-ended questions that encourage a witness to tell a long story. The concern is that if a witness is allowed to talk without answering specific questions some of the testimony may not be admissible and the opposing lawyer won't have a chance to object and keep out the inappropriate information.

*Relevance.* Evidence is irrelevant if it doesn't help the jury or the judge decide an issue in the case. An example might be a lawyer who wants to present evidence about how his client was abused as a child. This makes the client more sympathetic, but isn't relevant to a trial about an automobile accident.

**The Official Record.** Everything in a trial is recorded and saved for review. Any hearing or trial in a courtroom usually has a court reporter. The court reporter is an officer of the court who transcribes all the questions and answers, the discussions between the lawyers and judge and the rulings by the judge on motions and questions.

Increasingly, the court reporter uses audio or video recording systems to preserve the proceedings. The court reporter is an important part of the trial experience and will be typing a record of the trial on a special typewriter that requires specialized training. The primary reason the court reporter types even if the proceeding is being recorded is that the judge or lawyer may request clarification of a question or answer that was just given. Part of the court reporter's job is to be able to provide that information right away.

The impact of having a record being made during a trial is that lawyers and witnesses have to speak carefully and avoid using gestures to answer questions. Sometimes a witness will have to be asked to slow down or to say *yes* and *no* instead of *uh-huhs* or gestures like nodding or shaking their head. The purpose of these instructions is to make sure that the reporter can type what is happening as it happens and to ensure accurate recording of the trial.

**Judgment as a Matter of Law and Motions for New Trial.** At the end of the trial one or both sides can ask the judge to render a judgment as a matter of law. The basis of this motion is that all of the evidence has now been presented, and while a judge may have been hesitant to render a judgment before the lawyers argue that there is no real question of fact for the jury to resolve. Either side can argue that the evidence presented was clear and that the judge should make a decision, although the fact that both sides make this argument would suggest that perhaps there are still issues for the jury to resolve. This motion can also be made by the defendant at the end of the plaintiff's case before the defendant presents a case. Since plaintiff has the burden of proof and goes first, the defendant's lawyer can argue that plaintiff has not proved the case as a matter of law. This motion is often made and is usually denied.

Another motion, the motion for a new trial, is often made at the close of trial to request a new one based on some error alleged by one side or the other. This motion can be made during the trial when an alleged error occurs, at the end of the presentation of evidence or after the verdict has been given. The motion is rarely granted but may be if one side committed a serious breach of the rules and the judge believes it has prejudiced the jury.

**Closing Arguments.** The final act of the trial is closing arguments, giving the lawyers the chance to explain to the jury what the evidence means. The lawyers argue, express opinions and ask the jury members to render a verdict for their clients. Closing arguments are dramatic speeches where the lawyers get to explain to the jury what the trial was all about and what to make of the facts, the witnesses, the jury instructions, how the law applies and why their side has prevailed.

For the plaintiff's lawyer this is his big chance to explain how he has met the burden of proof and to talk about the damages that should awarded. For the defense's lawyer it's a chance to talk about the whole case or just the elements that the plaintiff's lawyer failed to prove.

Closing arguments can be emotional and passionate performances. The lawyers have great freedom in what they say, but they can only refer to the evidence that was allowed to go to the jury.

The plaintiff's lawyer goes first. Both sides are usually given the same amount of time to present closing arguments but the lawyer for plaintiff has two chances to talk to the jury so he will split his time. The defendant's lawyer follows the plaintiff's first closing argument. The plaintiff's lawyer then concludes the arguments with his final summary of the case and his request for a verdict.

**Instructions to the Jury.** When all of the evidence has been presented to the jury the judge reads the instructions that the jury must use to render a verdict. The instructions are drafted by the lawyers who submit the instructions to the judge based on established law and the model instructions for that state. The process of drafting the instructions is usually as contentious as the rest of the process. The lawyers are supposed to agree on the instructions but because of the importance of the way the questions are written the judge will end up resolving disputes and approving the final version of the instructions.

The instructions are usually long and legalistic, even though most states require that they be understandable. They're designed to help the jury understand what they're supposed to do, how they're supposed to do it, and what the law says about this type of case. See Chapter 17 for an example of basic instructions for a jury.

The instructions that present or explain the law of the case usually come from the statute or common law that created the claim in the first place. In the auto accident example, a jury instruction may be as simple as:

"Traffic Control Device Instruction: The court instructs the jury that the driver of any vehicle must obey the instructions of any official traffic-control device."

This means is a driver must obey traffic lights and signs.

Depending on the claims being made, jury instructions may go on for pages. In our accident example if one of the vehicles was a company-owned vehicle, legal instructions might include information about when an employer can be held responsible for an auto accident. If there are counter or cross claims both sides will ask for specific instructions to explain the law relevant to their claims. There will also be instructions about damages and legal defenses asserted by the defendant.

The last section of the instructions contains the questions the jury is to answer—the central questions of the case. Did the plaintiff prove his or her case? Are there damages and if so, how much? Some jury questions involve specific questions of fact that the judge needs to have answered by a jury before he applies the law.

If the plaintiff requested action by the judge, the questions may ask the jury to resolve the disputed facts so the judge can decide whether to take action. For example, if the plaintiff believes that a building was built on his property without consent the jury may need to decide where the property line is and whether the building is over the line. If the jury finds for the plaintiff, the judge can grant relief in the form of an order to move the building instead of awarding money.

**The Burden of Proof.** The burden of proof is the test or standard for deciding whether the plaintiff has won the case. A jury can't determine with absolute certainty exactly what happened in a case. Jurors may never know who ran the red light. The burden of proof is the test they use, and it is usually the plaintiff's burden to prove his case. There are three levels of proof used in trials:

**Beyond a reasonable doubt:** This burden is used in criminal litigation where the state must prove that the defendant satisfied each element of the statutory definition of the crime "beyond a reasonable doubt." It's difficult to put a valid numerical value on the probability that a guilty person really committed a crime, but some lawyers say that beyond a reasonable doubt means that the jury must be 98% or 99% certain of guilt.

**Clear and convincing evidence:** A few civil claims like fraud require that a plaintiff prove his case at a level of "clear and convincing evidence," which is a standard higher than preponderance (below), but less than "beyond a reasonable doubt." The jury needs to be convinced that there is clear evidence of negligence or fault, and, while hard to put in percentages, the standard is usually a 70-75% certainty of fault.

**Preponderance of the evidence:** If the jury believes there's more than a 50% probability of a fact, it's deemed true. In our auto accident case, if it's more likely than not that the defendant was negligent in causing the plaintiff's injury, the plaintiff wins.

## 9.8  Judgments

Once a side has won the case, whether by order of the judge or by decision of a jury the judge "enters" an order proclaiming the winner. The final judgment also states the relief—what the winner has won. The final judgment is the culmination of all of the legal proceedings that have occurred, although if the loser appeals it may not mean the end of the process.

Judgments come throughout the course of a case as well since any decision by a judge that resolves an issue in the case or the proceedings is called a judgment.

**Entry of Judgment.** When a judgment is actually written into the official court records by the court clerk, the judgment is "entered." The clerk sends a notice of the entry to each party. The date the judgment is entered can be important. If a party wants to appeal he usually has a deadline to file a notice indicating his intent. Some states require individuals to wait a period of time before remarrying after the entry of judgment for divorce.

**Default Judgment.** If a party fails to answer a summons or to appear in court when ordered to do so, a default judgment can be entered in favor of the other party. In a trial for damages a default judgment for the plaintiff will often result in an award of the damages requested in the complaint. If the complaint is not specific or if proof of damages is required the court may schedule a hearing on just the issue of damages. The defaulting party may be able to have a default judgment set aside if there's a good excuse for failing to respond.

**Summary Judgment.** This is when a judge makes a decision for one side and enters a judgment without a full trial. The judgment may be for the whole case or just to resolve a specific issue in the case. For example a judge may determine that the defendant really did run the red light and enter a summary judgment on the liability issues, but then allow the defendant to defend the case on the question of whether the plaintiff suffered injuries.

**Declaratory Judgments.** Declaratory judgment occurs when the judge declares the rights, duties, or obligations of the parties in a dispute. A declaratory judgment usually doesn't require action or award damages to another party. This is a common type of judgment in contract disputes where the parties know what they need to do once the dispute is resolved. For example, an insurance company may believe it doesn't cover a claim. The parties file for a declaratory judgment. When the judge interprets the contract the insurer will either have to pay or not.

## 9.9 Appeals

After the trial is over and the judgment is finalized by the judge, the parties have three options. First, They can comply with the judgment; second, they can negotiate a resolution that uses but does not follow the judgment; or third, one of the parties can file an appeal of the judgment. An appeal is a request to a higher or reviewing court for some change in the judgment or decisions made in the trial court.

**Appeal of Right.** Almost every state gives parties the right to appeal the decisions of a trial court. The first level of appeal is made to an appellate court that sits above the trial court but isn't of the level of the state supreme court. This appellate court may handle appeals for the whole state or just a portion of the state, and it is called by a variety of names and titles.

The key characteristics of these courts are that every person who's been a party in a trial has a right to have the appellate court hear his case, and that the decisions of this first-level appeals court can be reviewed by a higher court.

The appeal process is lengthy and requires very little from the client—just money. The appellate court's task is to review what happened in the trial and determine if there was a decision or evidence that violated rules or laws. Appellate judges don't use new facts and they don't hear evidence directly from witnesses.

When a party decides to appeal a verdict, the notice of the appeal has to be filed within a specified number of days after the entry of final judgment, usually two to three months. You can hire lawyers who specialize in appeals; appellate lawyers file extensive briefs and provide copies of the trial's official record for the appellate judges.

An appellate court is usually made up of several judges who review the long briefs and listen to arguments by the lawyers. Appellate arguments are prepared speeches made by lawyers. Judges interrupt as they have questions. The appeals court then discusses the matter and gives a decision, called an appellate decision.

Unfortunately, the appellate process can take years. Just getting the briefs and materials to court takes months and after the oral argument takes place the court may take years to make a decision.

Appellate courts can do several things. Most of the time, appellate courts uphold—or approve—the original decisions and judgments. In some cases, they will uphold a trial verdict but issue an opinion clarifying the law. And occasionally it will overturn all of or part of a verdict.

When the appellate court overturns a verdict the written opinion, or decision, will usually be longer since it explains the reasoning and gives instructions to the trial court.

Very rarely will an appellate court render a decision that overturns the trial judgment and creates a new verdict. Instead, the appellate court decides that the verdict was inappropriate and sends the case back to the trial judge with instructions to redo all or some portion of the trial.

For example, the appellate court may decide that certain evidence should not have been given to the jury and order the trial court to have a new trial. Or the appellate court may decide that the final judgment was calculated wrong and issue an order that the trial court should correct its mistake and create a new final order.

Appellate decisions are important because they provide guidance for all of the trial courts in a state on how to conduct trials. Published decisions become part of the law and are used by lawyers when they file briefs and motions with trial courts.

If a verdict is reversed, the party who won the appeal may have another chance to win in a new trial. But it has now been years since the original case was filed. Also, the side that lost the appeal can file a discretionary appeal.

**Discretionary Appeal.** After a case has been reviewed by an appellate court, the party who lost the appeal may try to appeal to a higher court, usually a state's supreme court.

A state's supreme court is the highest court of review, but few cases have a right to an appeal there. The party who wants to appeal must file a motion called a *writ of certiorari*. Based on those motions the supreme court decides which cases it will hear. If the court denies the request the appeals process is over. Most supreme courts accept a very small number of cases; sometimes as low as five to ten percent of the appeals filed.

The process for a supreme court is very similar to the lower appeals court; the parties file formal briefs and appear in court to present arguments. An appeal to a supreme court is a formal process and is taken very seriously.

The decision of a state supreme court is the final decision on issues of that state's law. The published decisions, called opinions, become the law of the state and are followed by all judges. A supreme court opinion is used by lawyers in briefs as they argue issues in courts at all levels. In theory, only a state supreme court can change previous supreme court decisions.

**The Federal Supreme Court.** The highest court in the country is the United States Supreme Court. This court is described and authorized by the Constitution of the United States and handles appeals from federal courts and occasionally from state supreme courts—but only if there is a question of federal law or a federal Constitutional right.

While people talk of taking cases "all the way" to the supreme court, the reality is that most civil cases can't go there. The U.S. Supreme Court only hears cases there are questions of federal or Constitutional law. When a case has a side issue about state law, the U.S. Supreme Court it is supposed to follow the law as decided by that state's supreme court.

For a case to be heard by the U.S. Supreme Court there has to be a constitutional question or issue arising from federal law or statute. If your case is based on a federal statute there is a possibility that you could get the U.S. Supreme Court to hear an appeal. Like state supreme courts the United States Supreme Court is a discretionary court that accepts a very small number of cases.

**The Appellate Lawyer.** Appellate work is very specialized and it's rare that a lawyer is good at presenting both to juries and to appeals courts. Appellate work requires great legal writing skills, knowledge of appellate courts and the ability to answer the questions appellate judges ask. If there's a lot at stake you should find a good appellate lawyer who specializes in appeals of cases like yours. If you're working with a large law firm they'll have an appellate department with lawyers who do this type of work. But it will take time and cost money for these new lawyers to become familiar with your file and prepare the appeal.

## 9.10 Remedies

Remedies are the solutions the legal system provides to the parties in civil litigation. Many lawsuits seek money, others seek some action ordered by the judge; money may not be an effective solution when trying to recover a unique item or seeking to have a contract enforced.

The law of remedies distinguishes between the three different kinds of remedies: Legal remedies, Equitable remedies, or Declaratory relief.

**Legal Remedies.** A legal remedy is when a plaintiff recovers or is awarded money for damages. Damages are paid to compensate the plaintiff for loss, injury, or harm suffered because of the defendant's actions.

*Breach of Contract*. Damages can be the amount the plaintiff should have received if the contract had been kept. Sometimes enforcing a contract is not possible so the judge awards money to compensate for the damages suffered by the plaintiff and to restore him to the position he was in before the contract was made.

*Breach of Duty—Tort*. Claims that arise from injuries from accidents or negligence. The defendant is alleged to have been negligent and is responsible for plaintiff's damages. Damages are generally awarded to restore the claimant to the position he would have been had the negligence not occurred. Damages in tort are classified under two general headings: general damages and special damages.

*General damages* compensate the plaintiff for non-monetary aspects of the injury, more commonly known as damages for "pain and suffering." Examples include physical or emotional pain, suffering, loss of companionship, disfigurement, loss of reputation, loss or impairment of mental or physical capacity, and loss of enjoyment of life. These damages aren't easy to calculate and may be subject to limits set by statute.

*Special damages* compensate the claimant for measurable losses suffered by the plaintiff. For example extra costs, repair, or replacement of damaged property, lost earnings, loss of irreplaceable items, and the cost of medical care. Special damages can also include money spent by the plaintiff to fix the problems caused by the defendant.

*Statutory Damages*. Damages that are created by a law. Violation of the law can entitle the plaintiff to specific damages as a statutory award. For example, a statute allowing the court to award a specific amount of money for violation of a law that injures a plaintiff.

*Nominal Damages*. Awarded to show that the loss or harm suffered was technical rather than actual. Usually a token amount awarded to acknowledge that one party is right, but the amount is so small that the victory can be said to belong to the other side.

The most famous nominal-damage award was the $1 verdict against the National Football League (NFL) in the 1986 antitrust suit prosecuted by the United States Football League. Although the verdict was automatically trebled as required by Federal antitrust law, the resulting $3 judgment was considered a victory for the NFL.

*Punitive Damages*. Also known as *exemplary damages*. These are not awarded to compensate the plaintiff, but to punish the defendant and deter other people from doing whatever was done. Punitive damages are awarded only in special cases where the negligent acts are considered egregious. They are in addition to compensatory damages. Punitive damages are rarely awarded but can be huge when they are.

*Restitution or Disgorgement Damages*. In certain kinds of cases, a defendant can be forced to give up profits made through his wrongdoing. The plaintiff receives as damages the amount of profit the defendant generated from the bad act.

An example would be using someone's intellectual property, such as this book. If you make and sell copies of this book with your name on it I can sue for damages, ask the court to stop your behavior and ask for all the profits you made from the sales. The idea is to discourage people from profiting from bad behavior.

*Legal Costs*. Generally a party is not entitled to recover the cost of its attorneys fees or to receive compensation for hardships undergone during trial. In some states there are rules that allow a party to recover costs for certain types of lawsuits or where specifically allowed by a statute.

**Equitable Remedies.** When a plaintiff wants the court to force someone to do something. Equitable remedies are always directed at a particular person or legal entity, such as a company. They're distinguished from legal remedies, because the court is being asked to make someone change their behavior. There are a variety of equitable remedies, but the principal remedies are below.

*Injunction*. An order where the defendant is required to perform, or refrain from doing, certain acts. If a party fails to obey the injunction he can face civil or criminal penalties and may have to pay damages or accept sanctions. In some cases disobeying an injunction is considered a criminal offence.

*Specific Performance*. This requires the defendant to perform a specific act. While a specific performance order can force almost any action, it is usually used to force a defendant to keep an agreement. An example would be an order forcing a homeowner to sell his home after a legal contract has been signed.

*Rescission*. Refers to the cancellation of a contract between parties. This is done to restore the parties to the position they were in before they entered into the contract.

*Rectification*. A remedy where the judge orders a change in a written document to reflect what it was supposed to have been in the first place. This usually occurs where the parties have made an agreement but have made an error in writing the contract, and one side wants to enforce it as written. For example, a seller and buyer agree to the sale of a car for $1,000 but write $10,000 in the price line. The seller has a signed agreement for $10,000 and would rather have the extra money, so the buyer asks the judge to *rectify,* or change the contract to the original agreed-on price of $1,000.

## 9.11   Resolution

Cases are resolved in a variety of ways. Remember that the point of a legal matter is to resolve a dispute. When parties work with each other to find ways to resolve their conflicts or arguments, lawyers and the legal system aren't required. It's only when two or more people have a dispute that they can't resolve, or where the government has an interest—like ending a marriage—that the legal system and the courts need to be involved.

Just because a dispute becomes a legal case doesn't mean that the parties lose their ability to control the resolution. In fact, most cases never go a trial; most are settled by agreement between the parties. The following sections briefly summarize some of the ways cases are resolved even after they've been formally started in the legal system with a complaint or pleading.

**Abandonment.** In some cases the plaintiff realizes that the case has no merit or that he or she cannot win. Sometimes the realization of how much time and money it will take to pursue the case convinces a plaintiff to give up the case. Since the plaintiff made the allegations that started the lawsuit, only the plaintiff can decide to stop the lawsuit. If the defendant tries to ignore the case the result will be a default judgment.

**Dismissal.** Dismissal is not really a method to resolve a lawsuit, but it is one of the ways litigation can end. The judge may decide that there are no issues to be resolved by a jury. Dismissal usually favors the defendant who files this motion to try to get the judge to decide that the lawsuit has no merit.

Filing a lawsuit has few barriers and judges don't review new lawsuits to make sure they conform to the rules, time limits or to check that the facts make sense. It's the defendant's responsibility to challenge the basis for the lawsuit or whether the complaint follows the rules or law.

For example, a plaintiff can sue for damages related to an auto accident whenever they want, but if the lawsuit is late it's up to the defendant to file a motion with the court pointing out that the deadline was missed.

In some cases, the facts aren't really in dispute. For example, a home owner sues his neighbor for damage done by a dog. If the neighbor can prove that he doesn't own a dog and there's no evidence he did, the case should be dismissed. The judge decides these questions and can dismisses cases after parties have had a chance to investigate and determine what the evidence is.

**Compromise.** The most common way for the parties in a legal case to resolve the issues is to reach a compromise agreement—a settlement. What normally happens is that as a law suit progresses both sides receive advice from their lawyers regarding the facts, the law, and the possible outcomes of the case. This legal advice helps the parties be more confident in their decisions. The evidence and circumstances of the case will usually dictate the nature of the settlement, since each lawsuit has unique facts and remedies.

The most common measure of damages is money so the most common measure of compromise is an agreement by one side to pay money to the other side. In a lawsuit alleging injury to the plaintiff the settlement is almost always about money—how much and how it will be paid. In divorce cases the issues are more complicated; money and the property from the marriage, custody of children and future obligations between the parties. In contract cases both sides are often seeking relief. In all of these cases the most usual resolution is reached through negotiation, leading to a final agreement to settle the disputes and end the legal process.

Compromise solutions are reached in a variety of ways. Sometimes the parties and their lawyers are able to informally discuss and resolve the various disputes and come to an agreement ending the litigation. But formal methods are used in many types of civil cases. These include mediation and arbitration.

*Mediation.* A process where the parties agree to meet and hire a neutral facilitator whose task is to help the parties agree to a solution. The facilitator has no stake in the outcome of the case and is often a lawyer or judge. The mediator usually has no force or power in the process, but a good mediator can be very effective in getting the parties to understand the downsides of continuing the litigation; and helping them find common middle ground for settlement or compromise of the disputed issues.

Mediation usually involves the parties and their lawyers meeting at a neutral location. Sometimes the parties will start by presenting their sides to each other but often the parties will go to different rooms while the mediator goes back and forth, listening to their positions and conveying offers and counter-offers.

Mediation is a very useful process and almost every case is mediated or has some form of discussion regarding resolution of the litigation. In many states mediation is mandatory and the judge requires the parties of every civil lawsuit to have some form of mediation or formal settlement discussion. In some cases, a judge not assigned to the case may act as a mediator, but more often, the parties will decide on a mediator from a list of possible candidates. The important characteristics of a good mediator are knowledge of the law, creditability from reputation and experience, and lots of patience.

*Arbitration.* Arbitration is a more formal process used to resolve disputes. In some states mediation and arbitration are the same thing, but in most areas, in arbitration the parties agree to hire someone to act as the judge and jury, making decisions that are binding on the parties.

The advantages of arbitration are that the lawyers have more flexibility in presenting evidence and arbitration is faster and cheaper than going through the trial process. A disadvantage is that arbitration is usually binding and the loser can't appeal the decision.

In arbitration the parties agree on a person or panel of people who act as the decision makers. In some cases each side will choose an arbitrator and the two arbitrators will pick a third so that the panel has an odd number. The lawyers or the arbitrators agree on how the evidence will be presented and the case is presented to the arbitrators; who give a decision to the parties. Arbitrators are often lawyers or experts who have some special expertise they bring to a specific case.

The facts and evidence can be presented like a trial or the sides can agree to provide written summaries of their case, called briefs, and the arbitrators review the briefs and make a decision.

Arbitration is a good option when both sides will benefit by having more knowledgeable decision-makers. Sometimes saving money is important to both sides, a huge benefit of arbitration. In other cases a contract requires the parties to use arbitration to resolve disputes. Many sales contracts require the purchaser to arbitrate claims instead of going to trial.

However, arbitration has a couple of significant disadvantages. The biggest is the loss of the right to appeal the decision; the loser is usually not allowed to continue pursuing the case. Another disadvantage is that arbitrators don't usually give out huge awards for pain and suffering if these damages are allowed in the claim. Very few personal injury cases go to binding arbitration because lawyers want a jury to increase the possibility of a large award.

In some cases arbitration is non-binding. The parties may want to get an assessment of how neutral experts would evaluate their case. In these cases the parties can present all or part of their case and the arbitrators render a decision, which the parties can accept or reject. Non-binding arbitration is usually a tool for getting the case resolved; especially in very complicated cases where the two sides can evaluate their cases.

## 9.12  Verdict

A verdict is a decision given by a jury or a judge. It's the least common way lawsuits get resolved. Less than one out of twenty-five civil lawsuits filed make it to a verdict.

The verdict is technically the determination of the facts that were in dispute in the case. It's used by the judge to give a final judgment which is based on the damages, the additional claims by the parties, the rules in making a final judgment, as well as the verdict itself. In addition to money awarded by the jury the winner may be entitled to interest, or the loser may be able to claim a reduction in damages because of previous settlements which the jury wasn't told about.

In some parts of the country the time from filing a lawsuit to end of the trial can be up to six years. The average is probably two to three years depending on the nature of the case and the city and state where you live. Some lawsuits take less time. Divorce cases can be handled faster, as can some of the other family and probate matters. But if there are serious disputes it can take years even with a judge who is trying to move the matter along.

The advantage of presenting a lawsuit to a jury is that you have the best chance for an unbiased group to resolve your dispute. But this is also the disadvantage of having a jury. A jury trial is the best system in the world for resolving conflicts between private citizens *if* there is no other alternative.

The problem with juries is that they know very little about the facts; if your lawsuit involves technical issues a jury usually has no special knowledge about them. Juries make mistakes; sometimes because they fail to understand the issues and sometimes because of the limitations of the legal system.

The judge carefully controls the evidence the jury is able to hear and see. This limitation often creates problems for the jury in understanding the facts and arriving at a decision. The instructions and the questions the jury answers are based on legal standards, and they're often not intuitive and are sometimes just plain confusing. Studies have shown that juries may reach the wrong outcome as much as a third of the time.

What this means is that there is no such thing as a sure winner in a jury trial. Any lawsuit can be lost, and any lawsuit can be won. The best lawsuit is one that would probably be lost at least once and maybe twice if you could try it ten times with different juries.

The advantages of a jury trial are that it provides a way to resolve a dispute that can't be resolved any other way and the losing party can file an appeal.

# 10. Criminal Litigation

*"Lawyers are the only persons in whom
ignorance of the law is not punished."*
Jeremy Bentham

## 10.1 Overview

The criminal legal system is very different from the civil system. It has its own rules and procedures and in many states and cities, different courts and judges who specialize in handling criminal cases. The criminal legal system is how government enforces laws and administers consequences and punishments to those who break the law.

Only the government can be the plaintiff in a criminal case. The person accused of a crime is always the defendant. Most cities or counties hire full-time lawyers called prosecutors who handle criminal cases. The federal government hires full-time lawyers to prosecute federal crimes. If you see a lawsuit where the "People" are suing a person it is usually a criminal lawsuit and the rules of criminal litigation apply.

Criminal procedure rules are the rules governing criminal proceedings. Most crimes are defined by local, state and federal governments through specific statutes passed by legislators.

Criminal procedure is subject to constitutional limits. The United States Constitution, with the Bill of Rights, provides basic protections including the right to have an attorney, the right to not testify against yourself, the right to question witnesses and the right to a jury trial, among others. A state constitution may increase rights in that state but it cannot take away from Federal Constitutional protection.

The criminal system is an adversarial system. Criminal procedure tries to balance the defendant's rights, the government's interest in an efficient trial and society's desire for justice. The rules of criminal procedure are designed to ensure that a defendant's rights are protected while protecting the rest of us from guilty criminals.

A huge difference between civil and criminal cases is that criminal defendants are entitled to be represented by a lawyer. If you're sued in a civil case you have no right to a lawyer. If you don't have one you'll either have to defend yourself or default in the case. But in the criminal process, the accused—the defendant—is given the opportunity to have a lawyer assigned for his defense at no cost.

## 10.2   Rules and Procedure

The rules of criminal procedure are the framework used to handle criminal cases. This brief summary provides basic definitions and describes the process most criminal lawsuits follow.

One of the most important principles of the criminal system is the presumption of innocence, a legal right of the accused. The concept is that no person will be considered guilty until convicted by a court. The burden of proof is on the prosecution, which has to convince the court that the accused is guilty "beyond a reasonable doubt." In principle, the defense does not have to prove anything. However, the defense may present evidence that shows that there is doubt as to the guilt of the defendant.

Another important concept of criminal law is that the crime or crimes charged against the accused have to be specifically identified. Crimes are defined by statutes and the burden is on the prosecution to prove all of the statutory elements (the requirements) of the crime. An important function of a good lawyer is to explain to his client the nature of the crimes he's charged with and to form a defense based on the elements of the specific crimes.

## 10.3   Preliminary Proceedings

**The Grand Jury.** This is a special type of jury used in some states and in the federal criminal courts to determine if there is enough evidence for a trial. Grand juries examine evidence presented to them by a prosecutor. If there is enough evidence the grand jury will issue an indictment. A grand jury is traditionally larger than the jury used during a trial. Only the prosecutor is allowed to present evidence to the grand jury; no defense is presented and the potential accused may not even know that a grand jury has been called. The primary function of the grand jury is to avoid misconduct by the prosecutor by ensuring that there is evidence of the charged crime.

**Arrest Warrant or Summons.** Warrants are typically issued by courts but can also be issued by houses of the United States Congress or other legislatures. An arrest warrant should be supported by an affidavit, which is a sworn statement showing probable cause that a specific crime has been committed and that the person named in the warrant committed the crime. An arrest warrant is usually required for any crime not witnessed by a police officer. But if police have reasonable cause a warrant may not be needed to arrest someone suspected of a crime. A bench warrant is an arrest warrant issued when someone fails to appear for a required court appearance or is in contempt of court.

**The Complaint.** The first pleading filed in a case by the prosecutor is the complaint and it includes the crimes being charged and the facts being asserted. It doesn't usually have to identify the evidence used to determine the facts. In most states the prosecutor has the ability to include less-serious offenses that could be charged under the same facts.

For example, if the accused is of murder, the prosecutor may allege both first-degree and second-degree murder. The jury will decide if there was premeditation, which is required to convict a defendant for first-degree murder. If the jury decides that a murder occurred but that it was not planned or premeditated the defendant can still be convicted of second-degree murder.

Criminal offenses are classified according to their seriousness. Many factors can influence the seriousness of a criminal offense. These factors include whether the defendant has a prior criminal record; whether the defendant committed the crime with cruelty, malice, intent, or in reckless disregard of another person's safety; and whether the victim was a member of a protected class, such as a minor, a minority, or handicapped.

Most states have two major classifications for crimes: felonies and misdemeanors. Whether a crime falls into one category or the other depends on the potential punishment. If a law provides for imprisonment for longer than a year, the crime is usually considered a felony. If the potential punishment is a year or less the crime is considered a misdemeanor.

Acts punishable only with a fine are usually not considered crimes at all, but infractions—like traffic tickets.

**Bail Hearing.** To make sure the defendant will appear at trial, the judge decides whether the defendant can be released and if a bond will be required to provide incentive to return. The judge will consider the weight of the evidence against the defendant, the nature and seriousness of danger to others in the community and evidence of the defendant's character. To decide whether the defendant poses a risk of fleeing the judge will evaluate the defendant's mental condition, financial resources, family ties, criminal history and how long the defendant has been part of the community

When a defendant poses a threat to the safety of the community he may be held in jail without bail. A defendant can be released without any required bail or he may be required to post a bond with the court in a reasonable amount to make sure that the defendant returns for hearings and trial.

Once the judge has set the amount of bail, that amount or a percentage specified by the judge is paid to the court. The defendant can post his or her own bail or find another person to do so. Once bail has been posted, the court issues a document—a court order—allowing the defendant to be released.

The penalty for failure to appear after release is usually forfeiture of the bond, additional fines, imprisonment or all of these. Once a case is over and all obligations have been fulfilled the bond money is typically returned.

**Initial Appearance/Arraignment.** After the arrest, booking, and initial bail phases of the criminal process the first stage of courtroom-based proceedings takes place: the initial hearing or arraignment. The accused is taken before the judge who is informed of the charges and decides whether there is probable cause to detain the defendant. The judge also asks the defendant if he or she has an attorney or needs the assistance of a court-appointed attorney. The defendant is asked how he answers, or pleads to, the criminal charges. His choices are guilty, not guilty, or no contest. The judge can also decide whether to change the bail amount or to release the defendant without bail and announces the dates of future proceedings in the case such as the preliminary hearing, pre-trial motions and sometimes the trial date.

The arraignment and bail hearing are often held at the same time. In some areas, and for less serious offenses, all of the initial steps, including the preliminary hearing (below), are handled at the same time.

**Preliminary Hearing.** This is where the judge decides whether there is enough evidence to force the defendant to stand trial. The judge has to decide if the prosecutor has enough evidence to convince a reasonable jury that the defendant committed the charged crimes. To reach this decision the judge listens to arguments from the prosecutor and from the defendant's lawyer.

The prosecutor can call witnesses to testify and can introduce physical evidence in an effort to convince the judge that the case should go to trial. The defense usually cross-examines the government's witnesses and calls into question any other evidence presented against the defendant, seeking to convince the judge that the prosecutor's case isn't strong enough and that the case against the defendant should be dismissed. Usually a preliminary hearing is a short process, but if the defendant wants to fight the evidence it can take several hours.

Not every criminal case has a preliminary hearing. Some states conduct them only when a person is charged with a felony. Also, if a state uses the grand jury process the judge may not be required to review the evidence at a preliminary hearing.

## 10.4 Preparation for Trial

**Pleas.** During the initial stages of a criminal proceeding, the defendant is asked to enter a plea or answer the charges that have been made against him. The choices are guilty, not guilty, or no contest (basically a guilty plea that doesn't require the defendant to admit guilt or have to tell the story of the crime). A defendant pleading guilty must do so knowingly, voluntarily and intelligently. A defendant can change a plea from not guilty to guilty at any time during the criminal process, but usually cannot change a plea from guilty to not guilty.

*Allocution.* To allocute means "to speak formally." In the criminal process allocution means that defendant must state specifically and in detail what he did and the reason for his acts in committing the crime. In most jurisdictions, a defendant is allowed to explain himself before sentence is passed.

Allocution is sometimes required of a defendant who agrees to plead guilty to a crime in exchange for a reduced sentence. The allocution can serve to provide closure for victims or their families and can help remove doubt as to the defendant's guilt in the matter.

**Defenses and Objections.** In preparing the defense the accused and his lawyer have several options. The best defense may be to present no defense at all since it's the prosecution who must prove guilt beyond a reasonable doubt. Sometimes the defense strategy is to attack the prosecution's evidence and witnesses, showing that the burden of guilt hasn't been proved.

But in some cases there may be defenses to the charges including: innocence, mistaken identity, or that the defendant was framed by another wrongdoer or the government. For most of these defenses the defendant's lawyer doesn't have to tell the prosecutor how the case will be defended, but some defenses require the defendant's lawyer to tell the judge and the prosecution that he plans on using them in the trial. This allows the prosecution to have access to witnesses or evidence needed to effectively deal with these arguments.

The following defenses require notice:

*Alibi Defense*. An alibi is a plea or defense where the accused attempts to prove that he was in another place when the alleged act was committed. An alibi is different from other notice defenses in that it's based on the premise that the defendant is truly innocent. In most states, the defendant is required to give notice of this defense to allow the prosecution to find and question the witnesses who provide the alibi.

*Insanity Defense*. This is an excuse defense. The accused usually admits that the act took place, but claims there is an excuse for the act. The defendant argues that he isn't guilty because he was mentally ill at the time of the alleged criminal action.

It's important to note that the legal definition of insanity in a criminal case is different from the psychiatric definition and the definition varies from one jurisdiction to another. When a defendant gives notice of intent to use an insanity defense the prosecution has the right to have the defendant examined by a medical professional to determine if the accused had the mental capacity to commit the alleged criminal act.

**Depositions.** Statements from witnesses taken under oath. They may be taken in criminal cases, usually with the permission of the judge. The reasons for taking depositions are different for each state. Most states provide that depositions may be taken to save the testimony of a witness. Some states allow them for purposes of discovery. The defendant doesn't have a constitutional right to be present at the deposition of a witness although such a right may be established by statute. A defendant in a criminal case may not be deposed without his consent because of his Fifth Amendment right to not give testimony against himself.

## 10.5 Trial

**Jury Trial.** Every person accused of a felony has a constitutional right to a trial by jury. The Sixth Amendment to the United States Constitution provides the right to a speedy and public trial with an impartial jury. The Supreme Court has also decided that a criminal defendant has a right to a jury trial not only on the question of guilt or innocence but also any facts that can be used to increase the defendant's sentence.

Jurors in some states are selected through voter registration and drivers' license lists. Forms may be sent to prospective jurors to pre-qualify them by asking questions about citizenship, disabilities, ability to understand the English language and whether they have any conditions that would excuse them from being a juror.

Only the defendant can choose to not have a jury, in which case the judge acts as the decider of fact and makes rulings on both guilt and sentencing. A defendant should waive a jury trial only on the advice of an experienced defense lawyer who believes there's a tactical reason for not having a jury.

**Defendant's Presence.** Generally the defendant must be present for every scheduled event unless excused by the judge. In some states the defendant can waive this right and choose not to be present at trial but the court cannot exclude the defendant from being present unless his presence poses a danger to the court or the defendant fails to obey the judge's orders. In some places courts use technology to allow a defendant to participate by video conference for some proceedings.

**Right to and Appointment of Counsel.** A defendant's right to a lawyer comes from the Sixth Amendment to the U.S. Constitution, which requires the "assistance of counsel" for the accused "in all criminal prosecutions." This means that a defendant has a constitutional right to be represented by a lawyer during trial. If the defendant cannot afford an attorney, the government will appoint one to handle the case at no cost to the defendant.

The accused has the right to a lawyer at every important phase of the criminal process, typically from arrest through the first appeal after conviction. The key responsibilities of a criminal defense lawyer include:

- Advising the accused of his rights and explaining what to expect at different stages of the criminal process.
- Ensuring that the defendant's constitutional rights are not violated through law enforcement conduct, or in court proceedings.
- Negotiating a plea bargain with the prosecution on the defendant's behalf.
- Investigating the facts and evidence, cross-examining witnesses, objecting to improper questions and evidence, and presenting legal defenses.

Defendants have the right to "effective assistance of counsel." Questionable strategic choices made by an attorney (and even serious errors in some instances) don't usually allow a conviction to be thrown out. It needs to be clear that the attorney's incompetence affected the outcome of the case.

**Opening Statements.** Just as in a civil trial, lawyers for both sides are allowed make statements at the beginning of the trial to set out the facts and explain what the trial is going to be about. The lawyers are supposed to avoid arguing what the facts mean since the facts haven't yet been presented, although both sides will attempt to describe the parties, victims, and actions in a way that helps their case.

**Taking Testimony.** The prosecution presents evidence first, usually through the testimony of witnesses, investigators, and experts to prove their case against the defendant. The prosecution has several advantages, including the right to go first and the perceived authority of the state, but they must be careful to avoid errors because the fairness of a criminal trial is a Constitutionally-protected right.

The defense lawyer will often focus his efforts on cross-examination of the prosecution's witnesses. Since the burden is on the prosecution to prove the guilt of the accused, the task of the defense lawyer is to find contradictions in evidence that cast doubt on the guilt of the defendant. In some cases the defense will also produce evidence countering the prosecution's case. The defense will also present evidence to support the asserted defenses of an alibi or insanity.

**Objections.** The trial's main purpose is to determine the truth between conflicting facts. Rules must be followed regarding how evidence can be presented, what questions can be asked and the how those questions can be answered. Lawyers listen carefully as the other side asks witnesses questions. If a lawyer believes that a question isn't appropriate, an objection can be made.

When a lawyer objects he has to explain the reasoning behind the interruption. The judge may allow the questioning lawyer to respond to the objection and then rules. If the objection is sustained the question isn't answered and the questioning lawyer will have to find another way to get the information he's looking for. If the objection is overruled the question is answered by the witness.

In criminal cases, questions about the evidence admitted can be very important because of the possibility of an error.

Some common objections include:

*Ambiguous, Confusing, Misleading, Vague, Unintelligible.* A lawyer can object to questions that aren't asked clearly. Both the witness and the jury must be able to understand the question and the answer.

*Arguing the Case.* Lawyers try to argue their positions all through trial. This objection is made most often in opening statements where lawyers try to argue the case before any evidence is presented.

*Arguing the Law.* It's the judge's job to explain the law to the jury. If a lawyer tries to explain the law or how it applies you may hear this objection.

*Argumentative.* An argumentative question is where the lawyer states a conclusion and then asks the witness to agree with it, often in an attempt to get the witness to change his mind. For example, "Based on what you saw, it appeared that the crime was premeditated—didn't it?" In this case, the prosecutor is using a witness to make a legal conclusion which isn't allowed; the prosecutor must show premeditation by the actions or statements of the accused, not the witness.

*Prejudicial or Inflammatory Evidence.* Judges aren't supposed to allow evidence that unfairly prejudices or inflames a jury. For example, a lawyer shouldn't be able to ask questions that might create the impression the defendant has a long history of prior criminal conduct, especially if that history has nothing to do with the trial. Questions about the history of a witness might be important but shouldn't be allowed to influence a jury when they have nothing to do with the trial.

*Assumes Facts not in Evidence.* Lawyers can object when the introductory part of a question assumes a disputed fact to be the truth.

*Calls for Speculation*. A question that asks a witness to guess is not appropriate, especially in a criminal trial. Witnesses are supposed to testify as to what they know from personal experience or expertise.

*Compound Question*. A compound question is two or more separate questions asked at the same time. It can be confusing when a witness is asked two yes or no questions, since the jury may not be certain which part of the question is being answered.

*Hearsay*. Hearsay happens when a witness tells the jury something said by someone else. For example, if one witness to a crime is asked what another witness said about it, that's hearsay. A witness should testify only about what he or she saw. If a witness were allowed to tell a jury what all of the other witnesses said the defense lawyers couldn't cross-examine them and the jury couldn't decide who was credible and who wasn't.

*Leading*. A leading question tries to influence the answer. "You sold the accused the weapon used to commit this crime, didn't you?" The lawyer shouldn't be doing the testifying. Leading questions *can* be used in cross-examination. In some cases, a judge also allows them with expert witnesses, with witnesses who have trouble testifying, and with hostile, evasive, or adverse witnesses.

*Misstating the Evidence or the Law*. A lawyer can make reasonable assumptions about evidence or previous testimony but will get an objection if the evidence or testimony is misstated.

*Narrative*. Lawyers aren't supposed to ask open-ended questions that encourage a witness to tell a long story. If a witness is allowed to talk without questions being answered, some of evidence might not be admissible. Also, the listening lawyer can't object to keep out the inappropriate information.

*Relevance*. Evidence is irrelevant if it doesn't help the jury or the judge decide an issue of fact, for example, a lawyer who wants to present evidence about how his client was abused as a child. It may make the client more sympathetic but isn't relevant to a trial about a robbery.

**Closing Argument.** The closing arguments are the final act in the trial and can be very important in explaining to the jury what the evidence means. In closing argument the lawyers actually get to argue, express opinions and ask the jury members to render a verdict for their clients. They are dramatic speeches where the lawyers are given the chance to explain to the jury what the evidence means, how it applies to the law as given by the judge and why that lawyer has prevailed.

While lawyers have great freedom in what they can say in closing arguments, they're still limited by rules, including the one that says they can only refer to the evidence that was allowed by the judge to go to the jury.

The prosecutor goes first. Both sides are usually given the same total amount of time to present closing arguments but since the prosecutor also gets to go last he may split his time. This is the chance for the prosecutor to explain how he's met the burden of proof.

The defendant's lawyer follows the prosecution and will use all of his time talking about the burden of proof and the failure of the prosecution to overcome doubts or holes in the case. He can focus on the whole case or just elements of the case.

The prosecutor then concludes the arguments with his final summary of the case and his request for a guilty verdict.

**Jury Instructions and Verdict.** The jury instructions are the legal rules that apply to the case and help the jury reach a verdict. As in a civil case, the instructions reflect the allegations in the case and the law that applies to them.

The difference is that the law in criminal cases comes from statutes passed by the legislature and each element of the crime must be proven by the prosecution. If a defendant is accused of kidnapping, the jury instructions will include the language of the statute that makes kidnapping a crime. For the jury to find the defendant guilty, each element of the crime must be proven.

The role of the jury is to decide the facts. Consider a case where a defendant is charged with kidnapping someone but the victim voluntarily went to the defendant's house, didn't try to leave and didn't know he was being held for ransom. While the judge will resolve the legal questions the jury has to decide from the testimony and evidence presented whether the defendant "forcibly abducted" the victim.

### Example Jury Instruction for Kidnapping

To prove the crime of kidnapping, the state must prove the following three elements beyond a reasonable doubt:

1) That the Defendant <u>forcibly abducted</u> and <u>imprisoned the victim</u> against his will. **And**,
2) The Defendant had no lawful authority. **And**,
3) The Defendant acted with intent to hold for ransom or reward or as a shield or hostage.

If the jury decides that the accused is not guilty of kidnapping he may still be guilty of a lesser crime as long as the lesser crime is also included in the jury questions. This is just an example; in some states, the victim doesn't have to know he has been kidnapped for the accused to be guilty of this crime.

The burden of proof in a criminal case is different from a civil case. The jury has to be convinced of guilt beyond a reasonable doubt. They don't have to 100% sure, but they are asked to be 99% sure of the defendant's guilt.

**Sentencing and Judgment.** In some cases the jury will be asked to participate in the sentencing phase as well. If the prosecution is seeking the death penalty the jury may be asked to render an advisory verdict as to whether the standard has been met for the penalty. Once the jury returns with the verdict the judge delivers the judgment.

In some cases the judgment is simply a summation of the jury's findings, but the judge has the authority to disagree with the jury if he believes that the jury was too harsh or that the evidence doesn't support the jury verdict. Because of constitutional concerns judges have limited authority to find that a more-serious crime has been committed but they can decide a less-serious crime has occurred.

After the judgment has been rendered the judge declares the sentence or punishment for the crime. Punishments range from fines, probation, jail or prison time, to the death penalty.

Most states use sentencing guidelines that give a range of punishments. The guidelines are developed by legislatures in response to concerns that judges have been inconsistent—one judge may put a defendant on probation while another judge would give a prison sentence for the same crime. Judges can deviate from the guidelines but must show good reasons for doing so.

**Double Jeopardy.** The phrase "double jeopardy" stems from the words "twice put in jeopardy" in the Fifth Amendment to the U.S. Constitution. This clause is intended to avoid repeated prosecution for the same offense.

Double Jeopardy offers three protections: protection from being retried for the same crime after being found not guilty; protection from another trial after being convicted – so the prosecutor doesn't try to get a conviction for a greater crime; and protection from being punished more than once for the same offense.

Double jeopardy doesn't address whether the crime was actually committed. For example, if police uncover new evidence proving the guilt of someone already tried and acquitted there's little they can do because the defendant cannot be tried again.

Jeopardy attaches, or is in force, once the jury has been chosen and sworn in. In a non-jury trial double jeopardy attaches when the first evidence is presented, which occurs when the first witness is sworn to testify. Even if the case is stopped before a verdict is given the defendant cannot be tried again for the crimes that were the subject of the trial.

## 10.6   Appeals

After the trial is over and if the defendant is found guilty, he has the option of filing an appeal of the judgment. While the prosecution can also file an appeal, the defendant is usually safe from being tried again.

A prosecutor's may appeal to have the appellate court rule on a trial decision so that the issue is resolved for future trials. For the defendant an appeal is a request to a higher or reviewing court for relief from the verdict or sentence.

**Appeal of Right.** A defendant has a right to appeal the decisions of a trial court. The first level of appeal is to an appellate court sitting above the trial court but on a lower level than the state's supreme court.

The appeal process is lengthy. The appellate court's task is to review what happened in a trial and determine if there was some decision or evidence that violated rules or constitutional rights. The appellate judges don't allow new facts or listen to more witnesses. In most states the defendant has the right to have a lawyer appointed to handle this first appeal if he wants one.

Lawyers for the defendant and prosecution file briefs and provide copies of the official record of the trial for the appellate judges. The appellate court is usually made up of several judges who review the briefs and listen to appellate arguments. The process can take several years.

Many times the appellate court will simply uphold—approve—the trial judge and the verdict. These decisions don't take as long to render. In some cases the court will uphold the verdict but issue an opinion clarifying the law. Occasionally the appeals court will overturn all of the verdict or part of it. These opinions will usually be longer since they explain the court's reasoning and provide instruction for a new trial if needed.

The importance of appellate decisions is that they provide guidance for all of the criminal trial courts in that state on how to conduct trials. Published decisions become part of the law and are used by lawyers when they file briefs and motions with the courts in the future. Very few appeals result in a complete change—a reversal—of the verdict. If there is a reversal the defendant may get another trial or be set free.

**Discretionary Appeal.** After a case has been reviewed by an appellate court, the party who lost the appeal may decide to take the appeal to a higher court, usually the state's supreme court.

A state's supreme court is the highest court of review but the right to an appeal at this level isn't mandatory. The defendant must file a motion, called a writ of certiorari and the supreme court decides which cases it will review. If the court denies the request the appeals process is over. Most supreme courts accept a very small number of cases, less than five percent of appeals filed.

The process for a supreme court is similar to the lower appeals court: the lawyers file briefs and appear to present arguments. An appeal to a supreme court is a very formal process; in many states only lawyers who have been approved by the supreme court can submit cases and appear to present arguments.

A decision by a supreme court is the final decision on issues of that state's law. Published decisions, called *opinions,* become the law of the state and are followed by trial judges and appellate judges.

**The Federal Supreme Court.** The highest court in the country is the United States Supreme Court. This court is described and authorized by the Constitution of the United States and handles appeals from federal courts and, occasionally, state supreme courts.

The U.S. Supreme Court can only hear cases with questions about federal law or questions that come from the federal constitution. In fact, when a case goes to the U.S. Supreme Court with a question of a state's law the Supreme Court is supposed to follow the law established by that state's supreme court.

For a case to be heard by the U.S. Supreme Court it must have a Constitutional question or an issue arising from a federal law or statute. The Supreme Court hears more criminal cases than civil cases because of the constitutional issues that arise from criminal cases. But only a few cases make it to the Supreme Court each year.

**The Appellate Lawyer.** Appellate work is a specialized legal work. It's rare that a lawyer is good at both jury trials and handling appeals. Appellate work requires legal writing skills, knowledge of the appellate courts, and the ability to handle the kinds of questions appellate judges ask. If there's a lot at stake you should find a good appellate lawyer who specializes in handling criminal appeals. If you're working with a large law firm they'll probably have an appellate department and lawyers who do this type of work.

## 10.7  Resolution

More criminal cases than civil cases go to trial, but just like with civil cases few criminal cases get that far. More criminal cases do go to trial because criminal defendants hope that the prosecution can't prove the allegations and because the only way to avoid jail time is a not-guilty verdict.

**Guilty Plea.** Every defendant has the right to plead guilty to the crime being charged. A guilty plea will lead to sentencing and final judgment and makes an appeal of the verdict almost impossible, since the defendant voluntarily admitted to the crime. A guilty plea may be preferable if it can persuade a judge to be lenient in sentencing.

**Plea Bargain.** A plea bargain is an agreement in a criminal case between the prosecutor and the defendant to settle the case against the defendant. The defendant agrees to plead guilty or no contest in exchange for an agreement from the prosecutor for more lenient recommendations of punishment. A plea bargain can also include the prosecutor agreeing to charge a lesser crime (called reducing the charges) or dismissing some of the charges against the defendant. In many cases a plea bargain is used to reduce jail sentence time or fines in exchange for closure in the case and not forcing the case into trial.

Sometimes a plea bargain requires the defendant to allocute, or admit the crime and tell the story of how and why it was committed. This may be required to reduce the risk of an error and to confirm that the person who is confessing actually committed the crime.

**Trial.** In almost every criminal case, the possibility of a plea bargain is discussed but in some cases, where the evidence is very strong or the crime is very serious, the prosecution has no reason to negotiate. Trial is always a significant risk. There's usually a bias that a person charged with a crime is guilty of something. Get the best criminal defense lawyer you can afford and listen to his advice when trying to decide whether to go to trial.

# 11. Organizing Your Litigation

*"The secret of all victory lies in the organization of the non-obvious."*
Marcus Aurelius

## 11.1 What to Keep

One of the byproducts of hiring a lawyer is large quantities of paper. Lawyers generate reports, notes, official pleadings and correspondence in every case—not to mention documents and notes generated from keeping track of and sending bills for legal services. A client won't receive copies of all of these documents but is entitled to have access to the lawyer's file and may request copies of documents. In the course of a normal legal matter a lawyer will provide correspondence and reports to a client as a matter of routine, although you have the right as the client to request as little or as much as you want.

One of the major themes of this book is client responsibility—your duty as a client is to be aware of what's going on and manage the legal process to ensure your satisfaction with the final result.

Keeping track of what's happening is crucial for managing your case and one of the best ways to do that is to spend time reviewing the documents you receive. Not all legal documents will make sense to you. You'll quickly become aware of how much is involved in a legal dispute. For lawyers these documents represent their work product.

Another part of your responsibility is to document your communications with your lawyer, including your understanding of conversations and agreements. If you have an important question your lawyer answers, get the answer in writing; even if just an e-mail. E-mail can be a great tool for creating quick and inexpensive documentation. If you aren't receiving any documents, you may ask your lawyer for the chance to review your file.

Here are some of the documents you should have in your legal case.

**Legal Product.** In cases where you hire a lawyer to produce a legal document, the documents you receive are the only documents produced and are the actual legal product you're paying for. Examples include wills, trust or contracts. When you hire a lawyer to prepare one of these documents, they should be kept in a safe location. In some cases you can ask the lawyer to hold on to the original for safekeeping.

**Correspondence.** Correspondence is a document sent between two or more people to communicate an idea, question or document something that has happened. These include letters, e-mails and memos. Correspondence is one of the best ways for you to see what's happening in the case. Letters to other lawyers will often include information about dates and events in the litigation or upcoming deadlines. To make sure you're aware of how your case is progressing ask to be copied on all correspondence. Make sure, when replying to an e-mail, your response does not go to the opposing side!

**Pleadings.** All of the documents filed with the court while it is in litigation are the pleadings. They are easily recognized because they identify the case, the parties and usually include names of the lawyers as well. Pleadings include the complaint, the answer, official discovery requests, your case's court schedule, and various motions and responses filed by the lawyers to move the case forward.

In most cases, pleadings are the least-interesting documents but they are important reference documents for understanding the decisions of the court and what's happening. It's always a good idea to get copies of official court documents, but it's probably not important to keep them in your active working file.

**Depositions.** Depositions are witness statements taken by lawyers with a court reporter present. These statements are transcribed and include questions and answers given by the person being deposed. The transcripts can be long, so depositions can be expensive to reproduce.

If your matter has lots of depositions you probably don't need to read them all. You may want to review the depositions of key witnesses from the other side in the litigation. Otherwise, rely on your lawyer to send you the depositions he thinks would be useful for your review. If you're curious, you can ask to review your lawyer's file for deposition transcripts. In addition, your lawyer may have had someone in his office prepare a short summary of depositions; these can be useful and you can ask for a copy.

If you want a deposition transcript that your lawyer can't provide, you can get one from the court reporter who transcribed the session. Court reporters keep copies of the transcripts for as long as the case is active. You should be able to identify who the court reporter is from the legal bills in your documents.

**Produced or Case-Related Documents.** These are the documents you bring to your lawyer. Many cases will have documents important to the case such as contracts, invoices, medical bills or reports that were created before the litigation began. They're collected by the lawyers. Always keep copies of every document you provide to your lawyer and ask for copies of any significant or important documents that the other side produces as well.

Be careful in requesting copies of all the documents in your lawsuit because there may be thousands and you don't want to pay the expense of copying all of them.

**Discovery.** Discovery documents aren't part of other document categories. They can include interrogatories (lists of questions the other side must answer), discovery motions and responses.

You may receive a copies of documents that are related to preparing for trial but don't clearly fit any document categories. Create a catch-all file for these documents. Sometimes, too, a document can fit into a number of different categories. The key to filing these is being consistent in how you handle them so you can find a document when you want or need to.

**Expert Reports.** In many cases both sides will hire experts to evaluate some aspect of the case, such as duty or damages. In divorce cases the parties sometimes hire experts to evaluate the value of property. In personal injury cases experts are used to testify about the accident, the negligence or the damages. Experts usually create written reports setting out their opinions and the basis for these opinions.

**Status Reports.** A status report is a special kind of correspondence that sets out your case's history, its status and the plan for moving forward. Some status reports will be short and about a specific issue; others will be broad overviews. Lawyers who work for insurance companies and corporations are used to preparing long status reports for their clients. Lawyers who work with individuals will not usually create the same kind of reports but will still report on important issues throughout the case.

As the client you can ask your lawyer to prepare a status report at any time, but if your lawyer charges by the hour you'll pay for the time spent on it. Status reports are useful and should be included in your working file.

**Bills.** Make sure the bills you receive for payment are more than just a statement or final number. Bills should include a summary of the work done, especially if you're charged by the hour. Make sure you communicate early in the case about what information you want included in your bills and how often you want to be billed.

The bill for legal work is the least favorite part of the legal relationship, but bills can be a good source of information regarding the case. Knowing the cost of the legal work can help you make reasonable decisions about getting a case resolved. Keep bills in your working file.

**Your Notes.** If you're a note taker you may find that you want to keep notes of what's going on and said in meetings and proceedings. These notes can be important for your own use. Be aware that in some states and for some kinds of cases, these notes can be "discoverable," meaning they have to be shared if requested by the other side.

There are rules protecting most of the communication between a lawyer and a client and the work that a lawyer does. But in some cases this rule will not protect your personal notes.

Make sure to talk to your lawyer about the notes that you keep and how they can be protected. If you keep a journal, talk to your lawyer about what you can write about the case and whether it will become an issue. Before your deposition discuss with your lawyer the notes you have and what you should bring to your deposition.

## 11.2 How to Organize Your Documents

Even if you decide not to get copies of most of the documents you'll still receive a lot of paper; including letters, pleadings and copies of the documents that your lawyer needs your help to complete. One of the most important keys to getting the result you want and keeping control of your legal case is spending the time to review, understand and organize the documents you receive. No single system works for everyone or every case, but some rules help everyone.

1) Keep too much rather than too little. Clients can be overwhelmed with the amount of paper they receive in a lawsuit or legal case. Avoid the temptation to throw documents away. These documents represent the legal work you're paying for. That doesn't mean you have to keep them all in the same place or carry them around with you wherever you

go. You'll never need to look at many of documents again and these can be kept in the filing cabinet in the basement or in a box somewhere dry.

Remember Murphy's Law—the document you don't keep, or can't find, will inevitably be the one that you need when a problem comes up.

2) Keep a small working file that includes the documents you need to refer to on a regular basis. There's no reason to lug around boxes of legal documents with you everywhere you go, but certain documents are important and you should keep them organized and easy to find. Your working file should include your agreements with your lawyer, status reports, and key depositions or summaries, plus any other document you think you'll need to find or refer to on a regular basis.

3) Organize documents *when* you receive them. Avoid collecting large piles in a single location, which will happen if you don't develop a system and use it as you receive documents. In my many years of working with clients I found that most of them resorted to throwing everything into a big box. Some clients even stopped opening letters and simply threw them into the box as well. If you succumb to this type of filing system you'll be engulfed by chaos. Trying to catch up later can become an overwhelming job. Don't let this happen to you; just find a system—any system—and use it.

4) Make notes on your copies of the documents. Unless you're holding onto an original document, all the documents you receive are copies. Don't be concerned about writing on them. If you call your lawyer about a letter or bill, make a note on that document to help you remember what was said. Limit your notes on documents to issues or actions regarding that document or you'll have a hard time finding your random notes later.

5) Document communication with your lawyer. Your lawyer will document most of his conversations with you and may send letters summarizing your conversations. When you have a question or issue document your understanding of what's happening and decisions or agreements that have been made. E-mail is a great way to follow-up with your lawyer. If you send an e-mail or a letter print a copy for your own records and file it with the other documents you receive.

Take notes during discussions with your lawyer. Include the date and a summary of what happened and what was decided. Notes can be kept in a separate file or in your working file. Don't try to remember everything that happens or is said.

When you have a question for your lawyer about a specific issue make sure you submit it in writing. For example, if you call your lawyer with a question about a legal bill and ask why you were charged for something that doesn't appear to be related to your matter, send an e-mail after the call summarizing the conversation. Put a copy of this e-mail into your file.

**Where to Organize.** If I were involved in a significant legal case where the outcome will have a significant impact on my life I'd use a locking file cabinet for the documents related to my case. A locked cabinet provides structure for organization and security for the documents. The drawers of a file cabinet can be marked and you can use hanging files with tabs to organize the various kinds of documents.

Other ways to organize your documents include binders, folders, or banker's boxes. Just be aware that even large binders will fill quickly and may require a lot of space. Whatever system you choose should be easily organized. You know you have a good system when you can find a specific document without having to look through everything.

No matter where you keep your documents make sure that it's a secure and dry location. Most burglars won't cart away piles of papers but since legal documents can contain sensitive personal information put them in an out-of-the-way place that's accessible and has enough light for you to file and look through them.

**How You Organize.** There are two ways to organize your legal case documents and you will probably use both. The first is by category or type of document. The second is in chronological order.

**Categories.** In a case of any size, you'll receive a variety of documents that fall into the categories described above. In smaller cases, you may not need as many different groups of documents, but most law firms organize and retrieve documents by type. Even in the simplest of cases there are four categories you can use: pleadings, correspondence, discovery, and bills.

If the case is more complicated, and depending on the kinds of documents you receive, you can use more labels or create subsections; such as depositions, experts, status reports and original documents. These different sections allow you to find specific documents as long as you can remember which section the document belongs in.

**Chronological.** The second method of organization is chronologically or by the time they were created or when you received them. The simplest system is to put the newest, or most recent document, on top or in the front of a section.

It's easier to file new documents in a file drawer or the folder at the front. When looking for a document go to the right section and look at the part of the file that corresponds to the time when you received it. It's also a good idea to write the date you received a document if it doesn't have a date on it, or if the date doesn't accurately reflect when you actually received it.

**Place Holders.** If you remove a document from your filing system, use some kind of marker to show where it goes. Colored construction paper is a good marker because it sticks out and you can write on it if you want to be able to remember what documents have been removed.

Keeping a file organized takes time, but it's well worth the effort when you need to find a document or are asked to reconstruct what happened.

## 11.3 Electronic Organization

With the increasing sophistication of computers and electronic document handling, there is no reason why your entire case can't be stored in an electronic format. Many of the documents you receive can be sent as a word processing or PDF document. If your lawyer lacks the ability or desire to create everything electronically you can scan the documents yourself. With simple hardware and software you can use a computer as an important tool to keep track of your documents and case.

**Receiving or Scanning.** Most of the letters you receive are created on a computer and can be sent to you attached to an e-mail. If your lawyer is agreeable and you have the technical ability this is great way to receive most of the letters, pleading and reports generated in the case. Some lawyers are concerned about sending documents in a format that allows changes to be made. Ask your lawyer to convert your documents into a format that doesn't allow the document to be changed; documents printed into a JPEG or PDF format cannot be changed and can be easily organized.

If your lawyer uses paper files (and many still do) they might not have the ability to convert documents received from another source—

such as from opposing counsel or a witness—from paper to electronic formats. In this situation you'll have to decide whether to store these documents in a paper file or invest in a scanner to create electronic versions.

Home scanners are reliable and simple to use. If you'll be using a computer to keep track of your case consider investing in a scanner with a paper feeder that allows you to scan multiple-page documents. Scanning long legal documents one page at a time is laborious and if you don't go crazy first, you'll probably end up with a perpetual pile of unorganized, un-scanned documents. The key to any filing system is to make it easy to use so that you'll be able to keep track of the documents.

When a document is sent in a changeable format, such as a letter in the original processing format, there's a risk that the document can be changed by the recipient. This isn't usually a problem but if there's a dispute later it's better to receive and send documents that can't be modified. When you send a letter to your lawyer send it in an image format. When you receive a letter in a changeable format it's not a bad idea to immediately change the document to a storage format that can't be changed.

Software and systems change so quickly that it is difficult to recommend one specific solution. Currently the simplest way to create a non-changeable document is to use a printer utility that creates or "prints" your document into an electronic format that is not changeable, such as PDF, JPEG or TIFF.

**E-mails**. Sending e-mail is a great way to communicate quickly with your lawyer, but messages can fall through the cracks in both paper files and electronic ones. Whenever you send or receive an email make sure that it's put into your file. You can print an e-mail or save it electronically. While you can create folders in your e-mail program to save e-mails, it's important to save a copy of them in your case file as well since e-mail programs can change and are not as likely to be backed up. This also helps keep them in the same place as the other documents related to your case.

**Folders.** As with paper files you should create electronic folders for the different documents you receive. An electronic system has several significant advantages and folder organization is one of the biggest. On a computer you can create folders and sub-folders allowing you to describe in great detail the type of documents in that folder. You can change the name of a folder or reorganize documents easily. You can keep copies of the same documents in different folders and easily send copies of your documents to your lawyer.

**Document Names.** An important element of a successful electronic filing system is the ability to find the right document when you need it. There are two ways to accomplish this: the first is using some form of database to index them and the second is to use descriptive document and folder names to help you to find the right document.

More sophisticated computer users probably have a database to organize and index their case documents so they can search and find the ones they need. The advantage of a database is the ability to use descriptive tags in addition to the document name. In a database you can create tags to describe who created a document, when it was received, which category it falls into and even summarize the document. The database usually allows the user to search for documents using any of these tags or descriptive fields.

Many people don't have a lot of database experience but they can still file and locate their documents fairly easily if they carefully choose their document names and file folder labels. These names and labels should provide enough information to distinguish them from each other. The name of a document should include basic information such as the type of document, the title if it has one and the date. In some cases you can include a descriptive word to help distinguish or identify the subject. For example, if you receive a letter summarizing recent discovery a good document name might be "DiscoveryStatusLetter11-01-12." If the letter summarizes the testimony of a specific person, you can include that person's name, "DepSummarySmith11-01-12." If you use a code, keep it simple—and keep a key to the code someplace other than on the computer. Develop your own system for labeling documents; just be consistent in how you do it.

By keeping up-to-date on entering documents into your system, using a folder system and choosing document names that provide detail you should be able to locate and use your documents when you need them.

**Document Storage and Backup.** Keep your paper documents in a secure, dry location. Back your electronic files up regularly. An option is to use on-line storage which provides a backup and makes your documents accessible from other locations.

**Original Documents.** Some documents should be kept in their original form, such as a contract or agreement with your lawyer. While you can scan a copy to your computer, keep the original, since it is the agreement. Sometimes you'll receive originals of orders from the court, and they'll be important to keep.

Ask your lawyer if you have a question about whether a document should be kept. Don't keep every letter just because it was addressed to you; this defeats the purpose of having a paperless filing system. Usually only a few documents need to kept as originals until the case is over and finding a safe place for those shouldn't be difficult.

## 11.4 Your Working File

Keep most documents in a safe storage place and build a working folder or file that's easy to use and transport. A binder works great as a working file because it can be easily organized. Even if you keep your files on a computer, you will find that there are some documents you'll refer to on a regular basis and want the paper copies.

These could include summaries, chronologies, reports and original documents that keep coming up as you work with your lawyer. Keep these documents in a binder that you can take with you to meetings. Your working file will be an important resource in keeping track of your legal case.

Resist the temptation to put everything into your working file. You won't need a lot of the material you receive on a regular basis. If you need to find the other documents they'll be neatly organized in your filing system. The real purpose of a working file is to keep only the documents you need when you're thinking about or working on your legal case.

Your working file can be organized into sections: your notes, correspondence, pleadings, discovery and bills. Keep track of your notes from previous meetings. You can keep your documents organized in chronological order in each section; or put a tab or label on each document for easy reference.

If you discover that you really don't need a document you've been carrying around remove it from the working file and return it to your other case document files. If you can make copies easily keep copies of important documents in your working file while leaving the originals in your file cabinet so you don't have to worry about replacing or losing them.

## 11.5 After the Case Ends

What do you need to keep when your case is over? After your legal matter is resolved you'll probably get a letter from your lawyer stating that he'll hold onto your file documents for some specific period. Some states have requirements about how long a lawyer must keep a client's file, while others leave it to the lawyer's discretion. Either way, a lawyer should let you know how long he intends to keep your materials and how he plans on disposing of them at the end of that time. If you're satisfied with how the matter was concluded there's probably no compelling reason to get the file from your lawyer, but you can if you want to.

What about all of the documents that you've collected and organized? How long should you keep them? This really depends on the nature of your case, but generally you can dispose of most of these documents when the case is over and you're satisfied with the result.

**Retention.** The only documents you need to keep are the concluding documents in the case and possibly some of the more important documents, including original documents and the original lawyer-retention agreements. If there's a verdict you may want to keep a copy of the judgment and the related court documents. If there has been some type of settlement you should keep the settlement documents and releases for your records.

The only time you'll want to hold onto all of the documents is when you're not satisfied with the work by your lawyer. The next chapter talks about issues that come up in the lawyer-client relationship. If you have any of these issues or problems the documents you have can be very important in evaluating how the file was handled and the appropriateness of the final result.

**Disposal.** Many of your documents contain private information so when you dispose of your legal documents make sure to do it in a secure way. Use a document destruction service or a shredder to destroy the documents before you put them in the trash. If there's any doubt about how your lawyer is disposing of your documents make sure that he's using a secure method to destroy them as well.

# 12. The Most Common Problems

*"Death is not the end.*
*There remains the litigation over the estate."*
Ambrose Bierce

Not every lawyer-client relationship is perfect. Lawyers and their clients usually figure out ways to resolve differences, but sometimes lawyers fail to represent their clients in a professional manner.

Remember that lawyers are people. The spectrum of their abilities and personalities is the same as the population in general. Lawyers have good days and bad days. They can be brilliant about some things and stupid about others. Many lawyers are driven to succeed; others are not. Some lawyers have great people skills; others are scary to deal with. You can have a productive relationship with your lawyer by staying focused on your legal problem and working with your lawyer to get to the best result.

Conflicts and issues can develop in any relationship. When you hire a lawyer you are the employer, even if you hired the lawyer on a contingency fee case. You are the client and the end result is the resolution of your legal problem. You don't need your lawyer to be your best friend—you need competent and efficient legal representation.

You may face some of the issues outlined in this chapter and they may be problematic and frustrating, but only you can decide if the issue is serious enough to consider finding and hiring another lawyer. For example, if a lawyer does a poor job of keeping you informed only you can to decide whether the problem is serious enough to get another lawyer.

Moving a case to another lawyer is a serious step. Lawyers don't like to be fired but they have an ethical responsibility to allow your file to be transferred. Getting a new lawyer will take time and add expense and it could create new problems as the case moves forward. But it's a step that you as the client and owner of the legal problem may have to take.

This chapter cannot list every issue or personality conflict that can arise, but it does try to outline some of the major sources of problems, frustrations and errors in a legal case.

## 12.1 Communication

The most significant problem that can happen in any relationship is a failure to communicate. In a legal relationship this failure can not only doom the relationship but also create barriers to achieving an outcome you can live with.

Most lawyers are decent listeners—listening is a skill necessary to the practice and the evaluation of the legal work they handle. Lawyers create problems when they're too busy or not listening to client's concerns and desires. They also create problems by assuming they know what the objective of a legal case is—which they usually do—but making assumptions can be dangerous for both sides.

Effective communication is making sure that you are heard and that you're informed as the case progresses. You need to be informed so you can make sure that the process is going in the right direction and so you can ask questions when unsure of the direction.

An important thing to remember is that **smooth talking is not the same as professional communication**. Professional communication tells you what is happening, what those events mean to your case and what decisions you may have to make. A professional is guilty of smooth talking when he tries to deal with problems or questions by making general statements and friendly assurances that everything is all right. The point of receiving information from your lawyer is to take ownership of the process.

The following guidelines can help you maintain appropriate professional communication.

**Time Equals Money.** When you ask a lawyer to increase communication, keep in mind that it'll take more time. If you're paying by the hour that means you pay more money.

Try to find a balance between what you have to know and what you can afford. As a general rule the simpler your problem is, the less communication you need.

Clients regularly ask their lawyer to answer unrelated questions or perform other legal work. This is fine if you understand that new matters require opening a new file and additional billing. Clients get upset when they're asked to pay for additional services but you need to be conscious of your lawyer's time. When clients expect or demand free services they risk becoming a problem client. Both sides should be able to establish expectations so that clients know what they're paying for and the lawyer isn't put into an uncomfortable or unprofessional situation.

A good lawyer can become a good friend if you work together for a long period of time or in several legal matters. To be fair to your lawyer and yourself, make sure you both understand when the clock starts and stops and when the personal relationship begins.

On the other hand, don't be surprised if your lawyer doesn't become as much of a friend as you think he should be. Many lawyers are careful to avoid socializing with clients because they want to maintain appropriate boundaries to the professional relationship.

Most lawyers sell their skills and knowledge in measures of time. Be aware that unwise or unfocused use of that time will cost you more and robs your lawyer of his most important asset.

**Establish Expectations.** One of the most important conversations you can have is about how communication will be handled. Make sure you both understand how information will be communicated, how your lawyer can get in touch with you and how often your lawyer will provide status reports. When you believe that there is an understanding make sure someone puts it in writing so everyone has a clear guide.

**Use Email.** Historically lawyers like to write letters, and their letters can be long. Many lawyers have come to prefer e-mail as a quick way to communicate, while they still use letters for some things. There are two reasons for this: concerns about privacy and concerns that e-mails can be changed. Both of these issues should be discussed when talking about using e-mail. Consider looking into encrypting e-mails to protect your communication.

More important are the security measures taken by both ends of the e-mail exchange, the sender and the recipient. If you share a computer with others take steps to ensure that only you can open and read the messages you receive.

For the same two reasons it's not a good idea to use a work e-mail address for legal purposes unless you're certain that your company is not screening or archiving your emails.

As a possible solution for the changeability e-mails messages request that letters be emailed in a JPG format, or that your lawyer send a paper copy of the letter later as a protection against unauthorized changes.

E-mail is a great way to engage in quick, concise communication. It lets your lawyer send documents for your review and participation in evaluating the case. Limit the back-and-forth that sometime occurs in e-mail exchanges and keep your e-mails professional.

While all correspondence is protected by lawyer-client privilege, anything you write could be seen by a judge so make sure that what you write in letters or e-mails is appropriate. When you reply to an e-mail make sure your response goes **only** to the people you intend to send it to.

There have been instances where clients have responded "reply to all" and accidentally sent comments to everyone in the original email—including the opposing lawyer! It's a good idea to ask your lawyer to send separate copies of emails and correspondence just to you so that you can't inadvertently send a response to opposing counsel or other parties in the case.

**Short and Simple.** Keep all of your letters and e-mails—and even your conversations—as focused as possible. Not only does a lawyer's time cost money but you'll find that when communicating with your lawyer you'll get a better result when you have an agenda and you follow it. Equally important is having your lawyer keep his communication with you focused on what's important.

Historically, lawyers must have been paid by the word, both spoken and written—that would be the obvious explanation for why lawyers take twice as many words as other people to say the same thing. Ask your lawyer to send status reports and correspondence covering only the important things like what happened, what he learned from it and what impact it has on the case.

Some lawyers like to prepare long descriptions of events that take as long to read as the original events did. Most lawyers working with individuals as clients know that clients don't want to pay for long letters, but if you hire a lawyer used to working for corporations you may need to remind him to be concise and less legalistic in his communications.

**When.** The issue of how often communication is needed can be another source of conflict. Sometimes lawyers working for corporations communicate too much, sending many lengthy letters and reports. Lawyers who work regularly for individuals can have the opposite problem. There are times your lawyer should automatically communicate with you, such as when something changes in the status of the case or when a date is set that affects you. But there may be other times when you want your lawyer to communicate with you.

One of the great frustrations for a client can be the long periods when nothing is happening. In some areas and with certain cases little happens until right before a trial or legal proceeding. These long gaps can be frustrating to a client, especially when there's no communication from the lawyer. Make sure you have a reasonable schedule set up for your lawyer or his office to send updates, even if it's just to say that nothing is happening.

It's also a good idea to have an agreement that your lawyer will communicate with you and perhaps get your authority before starting a project that will take a lot of time—and result in increased billing. In corporate work it's not unusual to ask a lawyer to get written consent for tasks that will take a certain length of time or cost a set amount of money. The written authority is usually just an e-mail confirming that you're aware of the project and agree to pay for the time to accomplish it. Good examples of these kinds of tasks include legal research, long legal motions or briefs. These are clear projects within the case and it's better for you and your lawyer if you communicate before you receive an unusually large bill.

When setting up guidelines be clear about the parameters. For example, if the cost of your whole legal representation is estimated to be $10,000 request that any single project exceeding $1,000 be cleared with you first. This may not stop the costs from exceeding your expectations but it can help you be aware of changes or significant work that's being done and help you to deal with expense issues as they come up.

**Associates and Paralegals.** In many law firms associates and paralegals do the day-to-day work on a file. Associates often appear in court and handle hearings and status meetings with the judge and are often well informed on what's happening in a case. It can make a lot of sense to receive regular communication directly from these other legal professionals. Partners want to protect their client relationships so even when a letter or report is produced by other members of your legal team the partner will often review it and sign it. Receiving communications directly from members of the law firm who are doing the work can be more effective and less expensive. Just make sure that it's clear who you're hiring and that your lawyer is involved in the important events and will be there to handle the trial or final resolution.

**Communicating with Your Lawyer.** Sometimes the problem isn't that your senior lawyer won't delegate any of the communication, but that he delegates *all* of it. Even if you have a good working relationship with an associate or legal assistant it's still important to have communication with the lawyer you hired to make sure both of you are on the same page and that your lawyer is still paying attention to the case. This doesn't have to be a monthly conversation, but even during the periods when little is happening try to touch base with your lawyer at least every other month.

**Written Confirmation.** You'll receive many written documents from your lawyer throughout the case and at times you need to respond in writing—sometimes in a letter, not just an e-mail. Remember that lawyers are very technical and if there's ever a dispute with your lawyer you may need to have written confirmation of an agreement or understanding to support your memory. Here are examples of the times where it's a good idea to put things in writing:

- **Verbal Agreement or Changes in Agreements.** If you and your lawyer agree to a course of action or agree to modify your relationship, put the decision in writing. For example, if your bill shows that an associate is charging the same rate as a partner you should call and the firm should change the associate's rate. You should then send an e-mail or letter confirming the billing change.

- **Change in Scope.** If the scope of the legal work changes and your lawyer does not confirm the changes in writing, you should confirms the changes. For example, you hire a lawyer to handle your divorce and discover some real estate issues that need to be resolved as well. If you ask your lawyer to handle these real estate issues you should send a letter to confirm what needs to be done and your expectation as to the costs and time. If you're wrong and put it in writing your lawyer will immediately get back to you. Don't find out later that your lawyer charges more for different kinds of work or that another lawyer in the firm is actually going to handle that part of the case. And don't be afraid to look for another lawyer with more expertise to handle a different kind of legal issue.

- **Concerns about the Case.** When you have specific concerns about how your case is handled put them in writing. Send e-mails or write letters if your lawyer isn't communicating enough, if the case doesn't appear to be progressing or when the direction of the case isn't what you want. The reason you need to put these concerns in writing is to make sure that the issues are dealt with and to create a record if the problems persist or if they don't get resolved. When an issue is resolved confirm it in writing so issues don't linger.

- **Resolution.** When you or your lawyer make decisions regarding final resolution, make sure that all decisions are documented. Your lawyer shouldn't make decisions about settling your case without your authority. Clarify your expectations when settlement or resolution approaches. For example, when you talk to your lawyer and he requests or suggests a settlement range follow up with an e-mail summarizing your understanding of the settlement process, the timeframe and the settlement that's acceptable to you. This protects both you and your lawyer who appreciates having his authority clearly defined.

**Dealing with a Poor Communicator.** While most lawyers are good communicators, some lack basic communication skills. You must decide whether your lawyer's communication skills are right for you and perhaps find ways to work around or resolve any communication issues.

One reason you might hire a lawyer who doesn't communicate well is that he's an expert in your kind of problem. If you have a huge contract you need written, a special kind of legal brief written or even some types of trial work you may find that the best-qualified lawyer for the work doesn't communicate well, has a huge ego, or is too busy to meet your other expectations. You can still hire this lawyer. The success of your relationship will be based on your confidence that your lawyer is skilled at what he does. Try to find someone else in the firm—an associate or a paralegal—who can handle the communication responsibilities. Sometimes you may have to be creative to deal with a difficult or odd personality.

Remember that you want your legal problem solved and it's your responsibility to see that it's done the way you want it to be.

If you've documented your expectations you can remind your lawyer of them. If problems become persistent you may need to ask your lawyer to meet to discuss them. Make sure your lawyer knows that there are issues that threaten to undermine your confidence in his legal representation—but only if there's a serious issue.

You can ask your lawyer to meet without charging you to go over relationship issues, but be well-organized and document your concerns in advance. You have the responsibility of deciding whether the issue has been resolved. Communication problems can be an indication of other problems, and if you can't resolve the issues, consider finding another lawyer.

## 12.2 Control

Another area of conflict that arises is who is controlling the direction of the case and what that means. Lawyers like to be in control and often think this is part of a duty to exercise legal judgment in pursuing a legal solution. To a client the difference between legal judgment and the responsibility for making decisions is often not clear and frustrating.

The biggest problem for clients is the lack of experience and knowledge of what to expect. For lawyers, control problems come from a variety of sources, but most often arise out of normal procedures of the firm and preconceived expectations. Lawyers develop procedures from expertise and out of habit. While it's probably not possible to describe every reason that control problems arise here are some common issues that come up.

**The Off-the-shelf Legal Product**. Some law firms are set up to deliver a specific product. More importantly, they deliver that product in a specific way. An example is an estate planning, "wills and trusts", law firm. The product they sell is well-prepared legal forms that meet the needs of most clients that come to their office. These law firms often don't have the resources, procedures or people to handle work that falls outside their area of expertise. Such a firm may be a great place to get a simple will or trust prepared, it may not be the place to have a complicated estate plan created.

Problems can develop when a law firm doesn't inform a client that a case or legal problem falls outside their legal product. The most common example is a firm that specializes in a specific type of personal injury case, such as worker's compensation benefits. The firm may be really good at handling one type of case but may not be equipped or prepared to handle other personal injury cases. Problems can develop when the firm agrees to handle a case outside of what they do and the client doesn't realize that they aren't the best lawyers or best firm for their case.

If you're uncomfortable with how the case is being handled talk to your lawyer and make sure that it isn't being handled the way every case is handled in that firm. On the other hand, if your issue fits the mold you'll probably get a good result for less money.

**The Lawyer Is the Expert.** Clients defer to their lawyers for decisions and strategy because lawyers are hired for their expertise. The lawyer is the expert, both in a specific area of law and in managing the legal system. Clients should rely on the knowledge and education of the lawyer in pursuing their case.

Your lawyer is *not* an expert when it comes to living with the result of your case. If you have concerns about how good your lawyer really is, you have options which can include consulting with another lawyer or even starting the lawyer-finding process all over again. But if the problem is really a disagreement about the outcome your lawyer is pursuing, the problem may be a communication issue. In the end you have to make the final decisions on how to resolve your case—you decide what outcome is acceptable. Listen to your lawyer's strategy advice but make sure your lawyer is working towards a final resolution you can live with. But if your lawyer warns you against a possible course of action you also need to be willing to live with the result if he turns out to be right!

**Unreasonable Expectations.** Most issues between lawyers and clients are the result of failing to meet the client's expectations. Sometimes however, it is not the lawyer but the client's expectations that are the problem. Clients have trouble understanding the limitations of the legal system and the restraints placed on judges and lawyers.

Almost every client will feel frustration at some point in a legal case and that frustration may have little to do with the lawyer and everything to do with the system. It takes years of experience to develop the understanding and patience needed to deal with our legal system; in fact, that patience is one of the things you should look for in a good lawyer. The legal system is complicated and the rules are often confusing; they may even seem counter-productive to justice being done. With regular communication, a good lawyer helps his client understand and prepare for what's happening.

Politics and judges will also impact cases. Judges are chosen through a variety of methods to make decisions and keep the system running. Like lawyers and clients, they come to the case with predispositions and ideas that will have an impact on the outcome of a case. Some judges dislike trying cases and will do anything to delay trials and put pressure on the parties in litigation to resolve it. Some judges, because of personal history or previous work experience, may lean to one side of a conflict or another. Judges can have agendas that frustrate the parties.

Lawyers have strengths and weaknesses that may become more evident as a case continues. At times your lawyer may be as frustrated as you with the court or with the lawyer on the other side. Lawyers are limited by the ethical guidelines summarized in Chapter 6 as to what they can do for clients or in the courtroom. Ethical lawyers try to avoid being a weapon for their clients; less ethical lawyers are less bothered by these guidelines. Think carefully about whether you really want to hire an unethical lawyer—imagine what can happen if you have a dispute with an unethical lawyer.

In the end, very few clients get everything they want from the legal system. Million-dollar verdicts are rare, and vindication is almost impossible. Every case can be lost. Juries and judges often seek a compromise of the parties' positions and the result is not what either side was seeking. A key to being a good client is having reasonable expectations about the whole process and taking responsibility for the decisions and outcomes.

**Ego.** Another control issue in a legal case can arise from the ego of the lawyer or the client. It may not be a surprise to many clients that lawyers usually have healthy egos. This ego—self-confidence or sense of importance—stems from a variety of sources. In some cases it's deserved, but only you can decide whether your lawyer's ego helps you or is an impediment to getting the result you want. It's not your responsibility to burst your lawyer's bubble of importance and in many cases doing so can hurt your representation. A lawyer's self-image is an important tool in the day-to-day conflict of representing legal clients.

The client's ego is a more difficult problem. If you're the type of client who's easily offended, if you want your version of justice no matter what or if you're incapable of compromise you'll probably have significant issues with any lawyer you hire. You'll also run into trouble if your case goes to trial since problem clients often present poorly to courts and juries.

A client's ego won't stop most lawyers from giving good representation. Problem clients only become a real problem for most lawyers when they cannot, or will not, pay for the legal services generated on their behalf. Demanding clients are fine but nothing is more annoying to a lawyer than a client who insists on fighting every battle and taking the case to the highest court, yet refuses to pay for the lawyer's time and effort. You are allowed to have a huge ego, but it'll probably cost you more money and it could make it harder to get to the result you want.

One last word on client ego problems: regularly ignoring your lawyer's advice will only hurt you. Your lawyer wants to win and the advice he gives you is for your benefit.

A classic example is preparing clients for their depositions, where the opposing lawyer questions a client under oath. Part of the preparation is helping the client understand what's going to happen in a deposition and how to answer the questions (*not* telling the client what to say).

You lawyer will probably advise you to listen carefully to the whole question, to answer just the question being asked and to not argue with the opposing lawyer. Clients with large egos usually ignore this advice and under the questioning of a skilled lawyer are encouraged to give long, emotional answers to simple questions; which hurts their case. Legal cases cannot be won in depositions, and your deposition isn't the place to justify or vindicate yourself.

---

**Lawyer-Client Rule Number 9**

Listen to your lawyer. Regularly ignoring your lawyer's counsel will hurt your result and the lawyer-client relationship.

**Conflict of Interest.** A conflict of interest is another reason for control battles and the worst of all possible situations for a client. A conflict of interest exists when a lawyer has competing personal or professional interests that prevent him from fulfilling his professional responsibilities to a client.

The most obvious example is when a lawyer agrees to represent another client with interests or an objective in opposition to an existing client's. Law firms perform a conflict check when accepting new clients to make sure that there are no conflicts with existing clients or matters. This is why you can't hire a lawyer in a divorce from a firm that your spouse has used in the past.

Other conflicts can exist as well and they are sometimes more difficult to discover. When a lawyer has a financial interest in an outcome that doesn't help the client there is a conflict. When a lawyer helps himself or a client at the expense of another client there is a conflict. When a lawyer maximizes his billing instead of seeking an efficient resolution there is a conflict. The difficulty in all of these cases is that the client may not always be able to determine when a lawyer has a conflict. It's often after the fact that a client may be able to figure out that the lawyer made recommendations or took actions that were in conflict to the client's interests.

If there is ever a time where you suspect a conflict in your representation find a different lawyer who can review the situation and advise you. With a consulting lawyer be clear that you're not going to hire him to take over the case; you're seeking assistance and advice on this limited issue.

One specific conflict that comes up most often is problems with handling a client's money. Lawyers are supposed to set up separate bank accounts called trust funds where client's money and unearned fees are supposed to be kept. When a lawyer mixes these funds with his personal or firm accounts or takes money without authorization this is a breach of ethics, a conflict of interest and sometimes just theft. Always clarify how your money is being handled if your lawyer is holding it and get a regular accounting.

## 12.3   Fee Disputes

A common problem in a professional relationship is a dispute over the amount of money that a legal case costs. Even when paying through a contingency fee clients can be surprised at the cost of a legal case and the money the lawyer gets for his services. While there are some things you can do to control costs, don't lose sight of your reason for needing a good lawyer in the first place—that you have a serious legal problem and it needs to be resolved.

On the other hand, if you begin to use your lawyer as a therapist or as a weapon in a personal conflict expect the bills to add up quickly. When you cannot or will not pay you create serious issues—and your lawyer will use the legal system to collect his money.

Here are some tips for avoiding disputes regarding the billing and fee aspects of your case.

**Set Expectations.** Discuss the costs up front and tell your lawyer from the beginning what you'd like to pay. Don't be afraid to ask stupid questions or appear unreasonable. Be polite but blunt in your discussions. Many times clients are surprised by the costs of a case because they didn't want to ask tough questions or appear not to understand what was going on.

It's all right not to understand, especially if you've never hired a lawyer before. If you're seeking a lawyer to solve a $10,000 problem, set limits on what you'll pay. If the lawyer you're interviewing cannot help you for a reasonable amount ask what other options you have, including other lawyers who may be able to help you for less. The more candid you are about the cost of your legal services the better prepared you'll be to make decisions and deal with the cost of legal representation.

**Get an Estimate.** After discussing the costs of your legal services make sure you get a written estimate of the costs and expenses. Make sure the estimate includes the time periods covered, the costs included by the firm and any caps on total costs and fees you discussed. Also make sure that any agreement or estimate includes provisions for what will happen if the costs exceed the estimate or agreement—how you'll be contacted and what your options are.

Keep track of the amounts spent and be willing to have additional discussions regarding your bills and costs of the case. It's possible to go too far in bill and cost control. Not spending any money will impact the quality of the legal work you receive.

**Understand the Fee Arrangement.** Make sure you really understand how your fee agreement works. The agreement you sign with a lawyer is a contract and you can and will be bound by its terms. A fee agreement should set out the rates of everyone working on the file, how often you'll be billed and what costs can be passed on to you as the client. The fee agreement is one of the important documents you should keep in your working file; ask your lawyer to explain and clarify the parts you don't understand.

It's also important to understand the terms and agreements in a contingency fee agreement, where your lawyer takes a percentage of your recovery as his fee. Some contingency fee agreements have a sliding scale of percentages, where the lawyer collects a higher percentage of the recovery as the case progresses. The lawyer may only get 20% of the settlement if the case is settled before the lawsuit is filed and may get as much as 40% of the amount once the case actually goes into trial.

You need to trust your lawyer, but realize that it may be in his personal interest to settle later in the process. Expenses are also part of the contingency fee agreement and all of the expenses incurred will be paid back by the settlement of the case. Make sure you receive information on how much is being spent in reimbursable expenses. Clients with contingency fee agreements are sometimes surprised with how little they receive of their settlement after spending years pursuing a lawsuit.

**Set Authority Guidelines.** When you set up your fee agreement, part of it should include some guidance on how large billing projects or expenses are to be handled. The idea is to make sure that you're aware of larger projects and expenses before they are incurred. Once you have some idea of the target cost of your legal work, set a threshold of any single legal project or expense amount and require notification prior to the work starting.

Sophisticated clients often require lawyers to seek authority before starting a project, spending money or traveling. These clients want to be able to explore other ways to accomplish the same project or work, or in some cases, may have already paid another lawyer to complete the same research or type of motion.

For most clients, having an authority level will help them know what's going on and can lead to meaningful discussions with their lawyer about other, less expensive, ways of accomplishing objectives.

**Time Is Money.** Every time you interact with your lawyer it takes time and time is what your lawyer is usually selling. Many clients are surprised when they call their lawyer to ask a question, share personal information or have a social conversation and are billed for the entire conversation. This is one of the biggest problems with going to a lawyer who is a friend before starting a professional relationship.

Friends who are clients also often want discounts that don't make sense for a busy lawyer. They don't understand when their lawyer friend doesn't have the expertise for their case or when the case isn't a priority for the lawyer. When dealing with your lawyer be aware of the time and resources you use—but be willing to buy the time necessary to move the case forward and resolve issues in your relationship.

**Review Your Bills.** Bills are a great source of information. You don't have to review every line of the bill, but take some time to be aware of what's going on and what you're paying for. If you're paying by the hour, make sure that bills are broken down to at least ten-minute increments. Tenths of an hour (six-minute increments) are even better.

Questions about a bill are perfect for e-mail, which gives your lawyer a chance to review the bill and his records before responding. Calling when you're upset doesn't usually help resolve questions. Occasionally errors are made in bills, usually clerical problems or entries put in the wrong file. If you don't review your bills you won't catch potential problems.

Even if you're paying on a contingent-fee basis ask for updates on expenses being charged to your account. These expenses will be counted against your final resolution and will come out of the settlement. Be aware of how that money is being spent.

**Pay on Time.** One of the best ways to make sure of fewer conflicts with your lawyer about fees and your ongoing representation is to make sure that your bills are paid on time. Nothing sours a legal relationship like non-payment. Lawyers have a legal obligation to continue to represent clients until the case is concluded or until they are released from that obligation by the court.

There are two primary reasons that a lawyer can be released from representing a client before his obligation is over: being asked to do something that violates the ethical rules and not being paid. Your lawyer wants to represent you to the best of his ability, but when it gets hard to collect payment his incentive to get the best result for you is lost. Pay your lawyer when you say you will, and if there's a problem, talk to your lawyer. Don't wait and hope that he doesn't notice.

**Work out Payment Terms.** If you have problems with paying your bills talk to your lawyer as soon as possible and work out payment options. Keep your agreements. If you're running low on funds it may be time to reassess your options and goals.

## 12.4   The Wrong Result

So what happens if you get to the end of a legal case and you lose? If you go to trial, losing is a real possibility. No case is a winner one hundred percent of the time and no lawyer should guarantee you'll win. Most solutions to legal conflicts leave all of the participants a little unhappy, but not always. At times there are clear and decisive winners and losers. It's not when a client is the clear winner that he or she will have the greatest frustrations with the legal system, courts and lawyers; it's when the client is a clear loser.

A client may not get the result he wanted for many reasons. Knowing them might not help the client feel better, but understanding the reality of a case and the options can help a client make better decisions as the owner of the case and the outcome.

**The Right Result.** The possibility that the right result in a case isn't a win for the client is the hardest possibility to accept. Hopefully, before a client loses he receives counsel from his lawyer that he might lose. Most of the time, juries and judges get it right—or as close to right as the system will allow.

Studies have been done of outcomes in legal cases and as far as the reviewers could determine juries are right around 70–80 percent of the time. Reality usually hurts, especially when clients and lawyers get too emotional about a case and lose sight of its strengths and weaknesses.

Good lawyers know that clients are a lot like children in their definition of fairness: fair is the outcome the client wants. Fairness, or justice, becomes a very personal and emotional goal that's not always possible or desirable in the legal system. That which offends or inconveniences one of us might not be the best basis for a law upon which to decide the rules for all of us.

I'm not trying to minimize the importance or harm of an outcome for the loser, but the law needs to be created in a logical context. The worst place to make up new rules is in a highly emotional or sympathetic trial setting.

An example of this would be the case of the landowner who builds an addition to his home. He discovers that he's accidentally built the new portion of his home several feet over the property line. The law requires the builder who built on another's property to remove the offending structure. For the homeowner with the new addition this is a harsh and expensive reality. A lawyer representing this client will argue that he believes that he's done nothing wrong, that he'll suffer an injustice and that there are "fair" ways to resolve the problem such as paying the reasonable value of the property taken by the addition.

But the law in most states requires the removal of the offending structure if requested by the property's owner. While an individual may have a sympathetic case and an unreasonable neighbor, we don't want to create a law or rule that could be abused.

Would you like to be forced to sell your property because someone built a home in your backyard while you were on vacation? In the end, the client who built on another's property will lose unless his neighbor is willing to negotiate a resolution. The home or at least the offending part of it will have to be removed.

Will the client be upset with this result? Yes. A good lawyer, understanding the law will tell his client that he'll probably lose. But that doesn't make a client feel better when he's paying a lawyer and then having to destroy part of his home.

The point of this example is that sometimes you'll lose because you are wrong or because the other side had the better case.

**The Wrong Result.** If juries and judges reach the right result more than 70% of the time it's also true that they sometimes reach the wrong result. If you're like most clients you skipped over the last section and immediately come to this section.

Please go back and read "The Right Result"!

You might not like it, but the odds are against you being that person for whom the jury reached a wrong result.

What does it mean that the jury got the wrong result? It means that there was a principle of law misapplied by the judge or the jury to reach the verdict. This is what is meant by the phrase "miscarriage of justice." **It does not mean that you'll win in the end.** But it does mean that you may have more options available.

You'll need a lawyer to help you decide whether there was a problem and whether you should appeal to a higher court. The appeals process is the way errors in legal cases are fixed in our court system. However, most appeals aren't successful because appellate courts have respect for trial judges and for the role of the jury in determining the facts.

The strongest appeals case is where a decision by the judge affected what evidence the jury was able to hear. If the judge decided that certain witnesses couldn't testify during your trial your lawyer may believe that this was an error. This is the kind of legal decision the appellate courts are more willing to review and may reverse.

If the appeals court agrees that an error was made you don't automatically win the case; you just get to have another trial. The second time you'll be able to use the new witness. Lawyers fight throughout the trial about what evidence can and cannot be given to the jury; they fight about what questions the jury receives and how much time they have to present witnesses and arguments. Most of the decisions a judge makes in these fights are "discretionary" and usually appellate courts are reluctant to second-guess how judges preside over cases.

The weakest appeals case is where you ask the appellate court to overturn the decisions of a jury. In the legal system the role of the jury is to decide the facts. When a jury has heard the appropriate evidence, judges who review the case are hesitant to reverse their findings.

If you believe that the jury was wrong you should have the case reviewed by a lawyer not involved in the case, preferably one who handles appeals. The appeals lawyer will review the case and give an unemotional opinion of your chances in an appeal and whether you should spend time and money. Your decision to appeal the verdict and pursue your legal remedies should be based on this evaluation as well as consideration of the impact of further litigation on your life and the cost of that litigation.

**The Weaker Lawyer.** Chapter 4 points out that it's better to spend some time and maybe even additional money to find the right lawyer—but it might not be until the end of the case that you realize that you didn't hire the right one. Using the term "weaker" is not an attempt to insult any lawyers, just a way to point out that lawyers' proficiencies vary because of their personal talents, knowledge, and experience. These differences can make a difference in the result that you get.

Sometimes clients have problems with their lawyer's abilities because they hired a lawyer they know or have used before instead of hiring a lawyer who handles a specific type of problem. The process of interviewing multiple lawyers and asking questions requires time and effort. Most lawyers can look like they know what they're doing for a long time. But when the lawyer has to perform it's harder to hide a lack of experience or confidence.

On the positive side, most lawyers who occasionally handle cases outside of their expertise usually advise and actively push for a resolution to the case long before a trial (or before the lawyer can be exposed). This is not always bad for the client, but it can be aggravating when you don't seem to have any strengths with which to negotiate resolution.

Another, less common, problem is when the lawyer on the other side is truly exceptional; a leader in his field with a reputation for success. This is problematic not only because of the impact it has on your lawyer but also because these reputations are usually deserved.

When you become aware that the other side has retained a "legend" you need to make some decisions. Will your lawyer's representation be impacted by facing this lawyer? Do you need to hire another legend?

There are two ways to deal with a legend. The first is to spend money and hire another high-profile lawyer; the second is to find an ambitious young lawyer who wants to be a legend and will be aggressive and fearless in establishing that reputation.

The decision to use a legend will have an impact on the cost of the case for everyone. Not only has your opponent decided to pay a higher fee for a lawyer, but the decision is also going to cost you more money; either in your own more-expensive lawyer or in the final settlement.

My personal experience has been that for the average client high-profile lawyers are rarely worth the extra time and the lack of attention that you'll usually receive. Most lawyers with good firms and experience will be able to represent you. What's more important is to find a lawyer who is committed to your representation and who will give you good advice throughout the process.

**The Unsatisfactory Negotiation.** Most cases settle without trial and that's usually good. Because no one can determine the outcome of a trial settlement is how the parties control the outcome and find, usually after a lot of conflict, a resolution that makes everyone equally unhappy.

But not all resolutions or negotiations are conducted on an equal footing and there are times when one of the parties is negotiating from a weaker position and feels enormous pressure to abandon a position or surrender.

The reasons for these inequities in negotiation are usually the same as the factors that affect the outcome of a trial. One of the parties has a weaker position in the case or there is a disparity because of the judge's decisions or the relative abilities of the lawyers.

If you've been told from the beginning of the case that you'll have problems prevailing under the law or circumstances, then the fact that you have little to negotiate with or about won't be a surprise to you and any resolution that benefits you is a good thing.

However, if you only realize during the negotiation process that your lawyer wants to surrender, you're justified in wondering about a change in his position and the effectiveness of your lawyer's representation.

**The Wrong Strategy.** Many times during a case, you and your lawyer will make decisions about how to proceed: which witnesses to call, what evidence to present and what claims and allegations you should make. All of these decisions can have an impact on the outcome and it may not be possible to know whether one strategy is superior to another. In fact you might never know if one way is better than another because you usually only get one chance to present your case and you'll lose or win based on the sum of your decisions.

Make the best decisions you can. This is easier said than done but some principles can help you. First, always keep the objective in mind.

It's easy to get distracted in a legal case by battles and conflicts that don't advance your cause or get you closer to the result you want. Don't lose sight of what you're trying to accomplish.

Second, avoid emotional decisions, especially ones based on anger or fear. Listen carefully to the advice you receive. When you have a neutral observer looking at your issues, such as a mediator or arbitrator, don't look for vindication or support. Be open to an unemotional and well-reasoned opinion and be willing to take a step back from the conflict of the case to get a better overview of what's happening and what needs to be done.

Your lawyer will make a lot of strategic decisions. If you lose, you'll probably question his decisions and ability. The test for those decisions is whether they were reasonable. Choosing one expert over another isn't a mistake; it's a strategy. Deciding how to pursue defenses or allegations is usually an important part of what the lawyer does, and again, even if it doesn't work out that doesn't mean your lawyer made a mistake or a wrong decision—or committed malpractice.

## 12.5   Malpractice

Malpractice clearly falls within the category of a wrong result. It's an important enough subject to merit its own section.

Malpractice, or professional negligence, is when your lawyer acts or fails to act in a way that falls below the standard for lawyers in a similar position.

It occurs when a lawyer does something violating the ethical rules, fails to do something that a lawyer should do or does something not for the benefit of a client and the client is damaged as a result. Malpractice occurs when because of your lawyer's actions you lose a legal right or outcome.

This section outlines the elements and issues involved in evaluating and determining if malpractice has occurred.

**Duty.** The first element is a legal duty between the lawyer and the client. If you've hired a lawyer and can demonstrate a client-lawyer relationship—if you've paid a fee or have a written contract—then there is a clear duty. Issues can arise when there's a question of whether a client relationship exists or whether a legal problem falls within the scope of a relationship.

For example, take a situation where a client or friend calls or casually talks to a lawyer about a potential case or is looking for a little free advice. The lawyer knows little about the actual case and the acquaintance relies on an offhand comment or suggestion. A deadline passes. The potential client then wants to blame the lawyer for the missed deadline. The lawyer is responsible only if it was reasonable that a person would think of themselves as the lawyer's client.

Another circumstance where this issue can come up is when you hire a lawyer to handle a specific type of legal case and then casually bring up another unrelated and different kind of legal problem. Does this conversation create a professional relationship for this second legal matter? Different states will have different standards but the general guiding principle is whether a reasonable person would believe that the lawyer was representing or advising him and whether the client's reliance on that relationship was itself reasonable.

For example, if you ask a lawyer about a personal injury case and the lawyer offers to take a look at it but you wait for a couple of years to go see him again, your actions aren't reasonable and the lawyer probably has no legal duty to you as a client.

**Breach of Duty.** Once it's clear that there is a legal duty through a lawyer-client relationship that duty must be breached to create malpractice. A breach of duty means that the lawyer fails to do something that a reasonable lawyer would do in that kind of case, such as failure to file a complaint within the time limits set by law.

If you have a personal injury case your complaint must be filed within a set period of time. When a lawyer files after that deadline and your lawsuit is dismissed it's probably a breach of duty.

A reasonable lawyer will file the complaint before the deadline, a reasonable lawyer will comply with court orders and a reasonable lawyer will comply with the rules of procedure and the ethical rules for that state. When one of these rules is missed or broken, a lawyer is said to be in breach of his duty.

It's important to understand that failure to win a case is *not* a breach of a lawyer's duty. In any case tried before a jury, one side wins and one loses. Fifty percent of all lawyers in trial are not committing malpractice simply by losing. In addition, clients can't second-guess the decisions and strategies used in a legal case after the fact. Hindsight is wonderful but cannot be used to decide that a lawyer has committed malpractice.

The *only* issue in determining malpractice is whether the lawyer's decision was reasonable at the time it was made. If a reasonable lawyer would have done the same thing there is no breach of duty and therefore no malpractice.

Breach of duty is established by expert testimony. The client can't decide or testify that what the lawyer did was unreasonable. Cases against lawyers require finding another lawyer willing to be an expert in that kind of law who will testify that what the lawyer did was unreasonable.

An exception to the need for an expert might be a case of clear intentional wrongdoing. If your lawyer steals your money all you have to prove is that the theft took place; most states won't require another lawyer to testify that theft of a client's money is a bad thing.

**Damages.** The third element in a malpractice case is proving that the breach of the duty resulted in actual damages to the client. Pretend you're a defendant in a criminal case. If your lawyer makes a mistake and one of the charges is not dropped, you have to be able to show that the charge caused you to receive a longer sentence. If the remaining charges would have resulted in same punishment it would be difficult to show damages.

In some cases, the result of a legal error is additional cost and time to fix the error in court. If your lawyer doesn't charge for fixing a problem he caused and you get a good outcome, you have no damages. If you *are* charged for the additional time and effort to fix the problem, the extra cost may be the only damages you have.

**Causation.** The last part of the test for malpractice is you as the client showing that the lawyer's breach of duty is what caused the damages you suffered. This is true in any liability case but in a legal malpractice case the test is a little different, because you not only have to prove the lawyer's malpractice, but also that the original case would have been won without the malpractice. This is called the case within the case.

**The Case within the Case.** Lawyers often defend their malpractice by claiming that the original case wasn't winnable. The client has to show that not only was there a breach in duty by the lawyer, but that the case the lawyer was handling would have been won if that breach hadn't occurred.

Let's say your lawyer forgets to call an important witness in a trial and that you lose the trial. You bring a lawsuit against your lawyer and you're able to show that a reasonable lawyer would have called this witness. As part of the causation requirement you have to prove to a jury that the witness's testimony would have made a difference in the outcome. A jury can decide that your lawyer was negligent and that there are damages from failing to win the case; but they may also decide that the underlying original case was not winnable and that simply having one more witness wouldn't have made a difference.

**The Professional-Judgment Rule.** The professional-judgment rule is that a lawyer has the right to make decisions within a broad spectrum of possible choices without being in breach of a duty to the client. The purpose of this rule is to make sure clients and other lawyers don't second-guess the strategy and decisions of a lawyer doing his best for the client. The client accepts the risk of bad decisions or bad outcomes when the lawyer is hired. This is why you need to take the time and make an effort to find the best lawyer for your case and why you should stay involved to the end.

## 12.6   Discovering Malpractice.

Clients know when their case has been lost but they might not have enough information to understand that there was malpractice by their lawyer. In a small number of cases lawyers actively hide their mistakes; more often a lawyer simply doesn't inform his client of errors or their effects.

The worst example of outright fraud I've ever seen in a case was where a lawyer continued to meet with a client and send status letters for a year after the case was dismissed because he missed a deadline. The lawyer tried to convince the client that the case had been dismissed by the judge after a year passed. The client went to the court to get a copy of the file and discovered that the case had been lost for more than a year. This is an extreme and very rare example, but it does demonstrate the problems clients can have because they rely so much on their lawyers.

So what can you do? The most important thing is to stay informed and take ownership of the legal problem and decisions. Read letters and documents. Be willing to ask dumb questions. Make important decisions and take ownership of the final result. If there is a question about something in the case make sure you understand what happened and the impact of the issue on the possible outcomes.

If you suspect a problem the first place you should start is with your lawyer. Ask what happened, why and how the event or decision has impacted the outcome. Don't be afraid to ask tough questions. Don't be afraid for ask for better answers; but also don't be afraid to trust your lawyer. If you've a had a good relationship, you've received good information throughout the case and you feel that your lawyer is answering your questions and explaining what has happened it's okay to trust your instincts and continue to trust a good lawyer who may not have achieved the best possible outcome.

# 13. Resolving Problems

*"If in your own judgment you cannot be an honest lawyer, resolve to be honest without being a lawyer."*
Abraham Lincoln

When problems arise in a case they can come from a variety of sources. Often problems are a function of the lawyer-client relationship and the solution simply requires discussion and agreement between you and your lawyer. Other problems are more serious and require outside help or action that only you can take.

## 13.1 Communicate

When a problem develops communicate with your lawyer. The key to resolving serious problems is to explain your concern or your perception of the problem as clearly as possible. Simply venting frustrations isn't helpful to the relationship. All clients get frustrated with the legal system. What you need to be able to do is identify a specific concern and whether that concern is related to something your lawyer has done or has control of.

For example if you're frustrated that your lawyer always asks the same questions and isn't listening to your answers—this is an appropriate concern to bring to your lawyer's attention. Give clear examples and if possible, use documentation. If you've received and sent numerous emails on the same subject send copies to your lawyer to let him know that there's a communication issue that needs to be resolved. If you have an problem with an associate or a junior partner, one option is to go to the senior or managing partner. On the other hand if you're dealing with the senior partner, going to a less-senior lawyer will only cause more problems.

Sometimes you may have concerns about some aspect of the case, but the problem is complicated by a lack of knowledge. Again, explain why you're concerned and your perception of the knowledge you lack in understanding an issue or making a decision.

For instance, you're concerned that there has been little progress for a long time. You can explain your ignorance of how long these procedures usually take and ask for clarification on what's happening and what can be expected. Be blunt but polite. Don't simply say, "I was wondering how much longer this is going to take." Instead, be clear: "When I retained you I understood that this case would take up to two years to complete. It has now been almost four years since this legal matter began and over the past year I've received four e-mails from you, but only in response to my inquiries. I'm concerned about the status of my case and would like you to explain why it's taken so long, where the process is at this time, and when you expect a conclusion (or trial) to occur?"

**Put your concerns in writing.** Take time to draft letters or e-mail. Make it easy for your lawyer to respond by giving him time to review the file. Create a record of your concerns, and if your lawyer calls you to respond ask him to follow up with an e-mail or letter summarizing his responses.

There are several reasons for documenting concerns and number one is to make sure that everyone in on the same page and that communication is professional and less emotional. Having your lawyer's responses in writing allows you to review them, make sure you understand them and confirm that they reflect your understanding of the issues. The other reason is that if the issue cannot be resolved, you'll want a record of your attempts to communicate with your lawyer about it.

**Be polite.** Assume that everything you write could become an exhibit for a trial someday. When writing to your lawyer about a concern or problem be aware that what you write and the responses you receive could be part of claim or complaint against your lawyer. This isn't to say that you should be sneaky or try to fool your lawyer—just that writing a long, emotional or insulting letter won't help you get the information you need and it won't make you appear reasonable to a jury at a later date.

Be as concise and clear as you can about your concerns and always stay focused on the reason you hired the lawyer in the first place. Don't try to sound like a lawyer or get too technical. Don't be tricky or distort the facts. The goal of communicating with your lawyer is not to prepare to do battle with him; it's to fix the problem so you can get the case resolved as soon as you can and with the best possible result.

## 13.2 Replacing Your Lawyer

If you decide you need another lawyer, act quickly. If the relationship has broken down to the point that you decide you need another lawyer the problems are probably not going to get better. Replacing your lawyer will take time and money, so it's not something to be done lightly. The process is similar to what you went through to find your first lawyer, assuming you didn't simply take a co-workers' advice and hire the first lawyer you interviewed. See Chapter 4 for the steps required to find a lawyer.

One positive at this point is that you know a lot more about your case, but there are still a lot of negatives about replacing a lawyer.

Most lawyers won't be happy about being replaced. If your lawyer appears relieved perhaps you've been a difficult and demanding client. Lawyers are usually hostile when being replaced and the only way to make sure that turning your problem over to a new lawyer happens in an orderly and professional way is to be focused and to not make it personal. Be clear about your expectations and be insistent—once you have told your lawyer that you have made the decision to replace him don't change your mind.

Hire the new lawyer *before* informing your current one of the change. Your new lawyer will need to be aware of the circumstances of the case and the problems between you and your current lawyer. If the new one has advice on how to move the file or how the change should be communicated, follow that advice.

Nothing sets off warning bells with a new lawyer faster than a client wanting to move a file and then refusing to follow simple advice on how to do it. Be aware that just moving a case will concern most lawyers—and potentially the court—that you're a problem client. You may have to take extra care to demonstrate that you're a reasonable and intelligent client.

Having a well-organized file and documentation about the problems you've had will help a new lawyer give better advice and get up to speed sooner. Your new lawyer will take extra time to review your file. This time and additional effort will cost you money. If you can't explain what your problems were and clearly state your expectations in the case many of the same issues might continue to be a problem.

Here are a few issues that you should be aware of when changing lawyers.

**Duty to Mitigate/Saving the Case.** The duty to mitigate is your responsibility to limit the potential damages from someone else's actions. This means that you can be responsible for some or all of the damages of a lawyer's negligence if you failed to take reasonable steps to resolve the original case.

Sometimes a client gives up when the lawyer relationship goes bad. Feelings of frustration from lack of control and a case that isn't going well can discourage a client from taking any steps to deal with problems or replace a lawyer who isn't diligent or listening. If a case goes badly some clients try to sue or pursue a claim against their lawyer, then find that *they* were as responsible for the result as their lawyer was because they did nothing to take control.

If you're aware of issues or problems before a case reaches its conclusion and you don't take steps to resolve those issues, you can be held responsible for that failure. Why? Because you are the owner of the case and the person most impacted by the outcome. You made the decision to hire your lawyer. You can be deemed responsible for the failure to make reasonable efforts to save the case.

Do what you can to get the original case resolved; a good result is much better than a possible claim against your lawyer. *Do not* count on the possibility of making a claim against your lawyer; that will be a much more difficult course of action.

A duty to save your case applies only when you're aware of the problem. If your lawyer has been hiding problems, you can't be held responsible for them. However, clients have been held partially responsible when they fail to keep track of a case or cooperate with a lawyer.

**Finding a Replacement.** When interviewing lawyers to replace your current one, be very clear about what you're looking for. Share the aspects of the case you want handled differently and what caused your decision to change lawyers. Hopefully you understand the problems that created the failure of the first relationship. Be aware of the status of the case and whether there are immediate time limits or dates your new lawyer needs to know. When you get a new lawyer communicate clear expectations: faster progress, immediate resolution, communication or anything else that's important to you.

One issue you may face is reluctance by lawyers to take over a case in the middle. Many lawyers will be concerned about why a client is looking for a new lawyer; they'll be concerned about possible mistakes or problems in the case and might be reluctant to take a case from a lawyer they know or have to work with in the future. Some will refuse to get involved; others will want to evaluate the matter and may need time to review the case documents and contact the court to check the status of the case.

You need to respect a lawyer's reluctance and do what you can to convince potential replacements that the problems were unique to your first lawyer and won't continue with a new one.

Avoid replacing your lawyer multiple times in the same case. You'll never get the result you want if you're continually bringing in new lawyers and eventually you'll alienate the judge.

**Barriers to Replacing Your Lawyer.** In addition to the reluctance of some lawyers to get involved in a case, there are two other possible barriers to hiring a new lawyer—procedural and contractual.

*Procedural barriers* exist in limited circumstances where for some reason the judge won't allow another lawyer to become involved in a case. This is pretty rare since an important principle of the legal system is a client's ability to choose his lawyer. But the judge can prohibit a change if he believes the purpose is to delay a case or frustrate the system. An example would be if the case is already in trial or close to a fixed trial date and the judge believes that the primary purpose of the change is to delay the proceedings.

*Contractual barriers* are more common and arise out of the agreement you have with your first lawyer. This kind of problem usually comes up when you pay the lawyer a set fee for a case or have a contingency-fee agreement. The issue here isn't whether you have the right to hire another lawyer but the impact on the fee agreement of changing lawyers in the middle of a case.

There have been huge battles between lawyers and clients in personal injury cases when the first lawyer claims his percentage of the final settlement. If two lawyers or law firms claim a large percentage of the final outcome there won't be much left for the client. Some contracts provide that if the client hires another lawyer, the first one will be paid for the work done at a high hourly rate but many contracts make no provisions at all.

In the case of a set or fixed-fee contract a lawyer may argue that he's entitled to the entire fee whether the case is finished or not. No matter what the specific issue is don't expect your lawyer to be reasonable when it comes to money. A lawyer who is fired will want to be paid what he thinks he's entitled to and that amount may be different from your expectations.

**The Problem Is You (or Your Case).** If you discover that you have many of the same issues with a new lawyer perhaps it's time to evaluate your expectations and your involvement in the lawyer-client relationship. You may be a difficult client or you may have a problematic case.

From a lawyer's perspective a problem client is one who makes the case more difficult by either failing to participate or by participating too much. A client who never responds to requests for information or who doesn't show up to appointments or court proceedings is a problem client. On the other hand, a client who requires too much attention and insists on specific results throughout an entire case can be equally problematic.

A good lawyer is patient with his clients and will be able to communicate his expectations. He'll let the client know when some aspect of the relationship is becoming an issue. A good client will listen and change his behavior when it's brought to his attention.

The other issue may be your case. For a lawyer cases and clients are closely related. If a lawyer isn't responding to your requests or meeting your expectations it may be because your case has problems which, hopefully, your lawyer has the courage to tell you about. Every legal conflict has two sides and both sides are not equal. Because of the law or the facts you may not have the better side of the dispute. It may even be likely from the beginning that you're going to lose. When a lawyer doesn't have the courage to tell a client that their case is weak and their chance of winning is remote, the lawyer often drags his feet in progressing the case. It's easy for the client to get frustrated with this lack of progress or results. Sometimes you have to face the reality that you're probably going to lose and need to do what you can to control the downside of a bad case through negotiation and resolution.

## 13.3 Bar Complaints

Each state has a state bar or licensing organization for lawyers. Each state has a discipline process. The scope of the disciplinary process varies from state to state but the basic purpose is to allow the state to take action against lawyers who violate the ethical rules of conduct.

The state disciplinary organization investigates and potentially takes action when a complaint is filed. Complaints or grievances can be filed by other lawyers, judges, clients or members of the community.

Examples of attorney practices prohibited by the ethical rules in most states include:

**Serious neglect of a client's case or the client.** Such as the lawyer's failure to file papers or documents with the court within required time periods, and an unreasonable failure to communicate with clients on a timely basis.

**Failure to account to clients,** as required by the rules concerning the status of funds or property held by the lawyer.

**Commingling of money,** or the failure to keep a client's money separate from the lawyer's personal or business accounts.

**Use of a client's funds** by a lawyer for his own purposes.

**Failure to put the fee agreement in writing.** This may apply only to contingent fee agreements where the lawyer's fee depends on his success on behalf of a client, but some states require all fee agreements to be in writing to help avoid disputes on what is owed. States disciplinary groups dislike getting involved in fee disputes and will help clients only if the lawyer has violated a rule requiring a written agreement between a lawyer and a client.

**Working for a client when there is a conflict of interest,** as defined and prohibited by that state's rules of professional conduct.

States have limited authority or desire to discipline lawyers for rudeness or for making an honest mistake. Their authority is limited by law to complaints about unethical behavior as defined in the rules of professional conduct or by state law. The most common problem that a state will deal with is inappropriate handling of a client's money or property by a lawyer, conflicts of interest and clear acts of negligence or client neglect. They don't want to get involved in personality disputes or allegations of negligence that aren't clear. Most states won't deal with cases having to do with decisions made by a lawyer who is otherwise in good standing.

States also deal with issues and problems arising out of substance abuse if they're discovered by other lawyers or clients and reported to the bar.

States encourage you to file a complaint with the enforcement organization if you believe your lawyer acted unethically. Filing a complaint costs nothing and you don't have to be a U.S. citizen to do so. When filing a complaint supply photocopies of any papers such as letters or canceled checks that relate to the problem.

Many states will review the complaint and decide whether to investigate it. If they decide to investigate the complaint the case is assigned to a staff member, usually a lawyer, to conduct the investigation. The lawyer is informed about the complaint and the upcoming investigation.

The discipline that may be imposed by the investigators include:

**Admonition,** meaning that the lawyer is reproved. A record is made of the admonition and printed in the legal journal of the state, but the name of the lawyer is not made public. An admonition will say that an unidentified lawyer was reproved for inappropriate behavior—usually describing the behavior but not the lawyer.

**Public Reprimand,** where the lawyer is publicly reproved and identified. Public reprimands are published in state publications that few read, such as weekly legal publications and may be compiled in the bound volumes of the state's permanent record or discipline reports.

If the investigator or investigating board determines that more severe discipline is required it sends the matter, together with recommendations, to the supreme court of that state. In most states only the supreme court can impose more serious discipline.

**Suspension,** or when the lawyer isn't allowed to practice law for a period of time. Suspension can be for a specified term or an indefinite period.

**Disbarment,** or revoking lawyer's license to practice. The lawyer's name is taken off the list of licensed lawyers. A lawyer who is disbarred can't apply for reinstatement for a specified period, generally from five to ten years.

**Restitution** of funds taken or used by a lawyer can be ordered as a condition for the lawyer to get his license restored and to be able to practice law again. However, an order of restitution is not an award of damages and cannot be enforced by the client. In some cases and in some states the only restitution that is ordered is the reimbursement of the cost of the state's investigation and the client is left to pursue other means of collecting damages that occurred from the alleged breach.

In some cases a lawyer may resign rather than face disciplinary action, but that usually requires the bar or supreme court's consent. Decisions of the investigating board or the court with respect to public discipline are released for publication.

The lawyers who investigate your complaint don't represent you personally, so you shouldn't expect the state to provide legal services or advice. While complaints are taken seriously, their concern is about ethical breaches and protecting lawyers as well as clients. Complaints are usually confidential. Until the lawyer has been served with a petition for discipline instituting formal charges or has agreed to be formally disciplined after the initial investigation the state won't usually publicly disclose that the complaint has been filed.

The complaint process can be frustrating. Very few lawyers are disbarred or even suspended. The process provides little relief for the client as the state has little authority to provide relief and it's mostly concerned with the ethical rules.

Even so, when a lawyer has broken a rule it's important for the reputation of the state's legal system and future clients to report the problem. You might not get anything out of the process, but you can help solve serious future problems. A lawyer isn't allowed to retaliate when a client files a complaint. As a client you're immune from liability, which means your lawyer cannot sue you for making a complaint in good faith.

## 13.4  Suing Your Lawyer

If your lawyer has broken an ethical rule or been negligent and you've been damaged by that negligence you have the option of suing. A lawsuit against a lawyer who has represented you is a unique experience—and can be an unpleasant one. But it may be the only way to protect your interests if your matter has been mishandled and it has cost you money or you have suffered some other damage.

To sue your lawyer, you need a lawyer. Finding someone specializing in lawyer malpractice can be difficult. In each state only a few lawyers do so. It's possible that the state licensing organization or bar organizations can give you the name of lawyers who handle legal malpractice cases.

If you have been consulting with a lawyer or have hired a new lawyer, he may be able to provide a referral or make a recommendation. Another way to find someone who handles these cases may be a referral web site, where lawyers are listed by specialty. Interview several potential lawyers and make a decision based on what you learn in the interviews, the recommendations you have received and your experiences. Most lawyers who handle these cases will use a contingent fee arrangement, meaning that the lawyer will be paid a percentage of the final recovery. This can be an advantage because you don't have to pay fees as the case progresses and you won't have to pay the lawyer if you lose. But it also means that if you win just enough to be made whole your lawyer will get twenty or forty percent of the final recovery.

Once you have a lawyer and a retention agreement in place, you need to be aware of some issues in pursuing a claim against a lawyer.

**The Case within a Case.** When suing a lawyer, you really have to win two cases; that's why professionals who deal with lawyer malpractice often talk about the "case within a case" requirement. Not only do you have to show that the lawyer failed to handle your representation in a professional manner, you also have to prove that your underlying case was winnable. The following examples explain how this works.

In a simple case, your lawyer failed to file an answer within the time limit so you lost the case. It's easy to show that the lawyer was negligent because a reasonable lawyer files answers within the applicable time limits. However, just knowing the lawyer was negligent doesn't mean you win. You still have to show that the original case would have been won if the lawyer hadn't missed the deadline. If your original lawyer can prove that the original case didn't have merit you'll lose because you have no damages if you had an unwinnable case.

It becomes more difficult to prove malpractice when the lawyer's acts weren't clearly negligent. For example, if your lawyer wasn't aware of an appellate case that holds against your position so you lose your lawsuit. Your lawyer may defend himself that under the circumstances, it wasn't unreasonable that he was unaware of the other case. Then he can use that same appellate decision to show that you couldn't have prevailed in your lawsuit no matter what he did.

The point here—you need to evaluate the strength of both the case against the lawyer *and* the strength of the original case that was lost in order to be successful in pursuing a malpractice case.

**Lack of Confidentiality.** When you hire a lawyer, all of the information you reveal or discuss is confidential. With very few exceptions your lawyer cannot discuss or reveal what you've told him in the course of your lawyer-client relationship. One of those exceptions is when he's sued by a client. This should affect you only if there are facts your lawyer knew that would have had an impact on your ability to win the case. Some lawyers will seek to divulge everything as a defense, or even a weapon, when they're sued.

A good lawyer who handles legal malpractice cases will minimize the impact of embarrassing personal information that your former lawyer knows, but in order to protect you your malpractice case lawyer needs to know in advance what those facts are. A lawyer can ask the court to protect embarrassing information only if it really has nothing to do with the case.

The kinds of facts that may be difficult to keep confidential are those that show a lack of honesty, those that involve fraud being committed and facts regarding responsibility or even guilt in the underlying case.

**Increased Hurdles.** Another unique aspect of a lawyer malpractice case is that there are so many lawyers involved. The defendant is a lawyer, he will hire a lawyer to defend himself, you will have a lawyer, the judge will be a lawyer and all of the experts hired to render opinions are lawyers. You as the client may feel left out as the only non-lawyer in the process.

One great disadvantage for you in suing a lawyer in a malpractice case is that judge is more inclined to dismiss it or rule in favor of the lawyer defendant. This isn't because the judge favors lawyers, but because a judge has practiced law and better understands the issues and standards in a lawyer malpractice case than in other types of cases.

For example, in a negligence case against a doctor the doctor may have better experts and defenses, but the judge won't feel qualified to decide which of the experts—who are all doctors—is most credible. When a malpractice lawsuit involves a lawyer, the judge is more comfortable making these decisions. More cases against lawyers are dismissed by the court then for almost any other type of professional liability lawsuit.

This is not to discourage you from pursuing a lawsuit against a lawyer who has committed malpractice. Just be aware of some of the special problems you'll face in winning your case. If your lawyer has failed to do something or has done something he shouldn't have and you've been injured because of his negligence, a lawsuit may be the best option available and the only way to be made whole. Some lawsuits against lawyers *are* very successful. To get a good result you'll need to be patient and persistent.

One last note—if you interview several different lawyers who regularly handle lawyer malpractice litigation and they all refuse to represent you, that's a good sign that you don't have a good case. Lawyers taking these cases won't help you get revenge; they're concerned about winning the case and recovering enough money to pay the costs and justify the lawsuit. It's usually *not* a good idea to hire a lawyer without malpractice experience and it's very difficult to represent yourself in a lawsuit against a lawyer. I've never seen a client win a lawsuit against a lawyer when representing himself.

# 14. Conclusion

*"Discourage litigation. Persuade your neighbors to compromise whenever you can. As a peacemaker the lawyer has superior opportunity of being a good man. There will still be business enough."*
Abraham Lincoln

If you've read this book from cover to cover, this chapter won't have any new information. If you've skipped to the final chapter, don't worry . . I won't give away the plot! This chapter is to remind you of a few points and give you some hope.

Hiring a lawyer isn't as daunting or as frustrating as it may seem. Most lawyer-client relationships work well and require minor adjustments as lawyers and clients communicate and work towards a common solution.

You hire a lawyer to help solve a legal problem, but no lawyer can change reality. Lawyers are an expensive way to get revenge and lawyers make lousy therapists.

For the conclusion, here are some last thoughts on the rules set out throughout the book.

> **Lawyer-Client Rule Number 1 . . . Page 4**
>
> You are hiring a lawyer to solve *your* legal problem. You have to live with the final result. Don't abandon your responsibility for the outcome to your lawyer or to the system.

You have a legal problem and have decided you need a lawyer. This book is *not* for those who want to represent themselves or learn the law. It's a guidebook to help find the right lawyer and get the best possible result.

The legal problem that makes getting a lawyer necessary is yours. When the case is over your lawyer will go back to practicing law and you'll have to live with the results you purchased.

When you have a dispute, a legal problem, or a conflict, the first thing you need to decide is what the best result would be for you. If you're the person wanting to file a lawsuit make sure it makes sense to get a lawyer in the first place. I have advised clients that a lawsuit was *not* their best option, that the legal process would be expensive and wouldn't help and that even if winning were likely it wouldn't help the clients get on with their lives.

Try to avoid getting emotional when you make these decisions. The legal system is not a game, it's not a contest. There are no prizes for Client of the Year. The odds are against winning a lottery-type verdict or getting everything you want.

Take responsibility for managing your case, make the tough decisions, and be willing to live with the result.

---
**Lawyer-Client Rule Number 2 . . . Page 10**

Don't be intimidated by lawyers. Knowing how lawyers are educated and licensed will help you to see them as people. Lawyers are subject to all of the same problems and motivations as the rest of us.

---

When you're involved in a legal problem that involves other parties and other lawyers one of the things that can be overwhelming is the number of lawyers you have to deal with. This can really be noticeable when you are in an official proceeding or process like a deposition.

Remember that lawyers are simply overeducated people with a unique education and work experience. If a lawyer intimidates you—even your own lawyer—it's in large part because you let them.

Some lawyers are aggressive and may be even abusively overbearing. Abusive lawyers often make threats to try to take advantage of your lack of knowledge about the law. If a lawyer is making threats don't get upset. Don't trust a threatening lawyer to explain your options or to be concerned about your welfare. Request that all communication be in writing and force him to create a record that can be reviewed by other lawyers, the judge or a state disciplinary board.

The best way to protect yourself from an aggressive lawyer is to hire a lawyer to represent you and deal with the aggression and assertions being made against you. If you find that the opposing lawyer is overly aggressive follow your lawyer's counsel on how to respond. If you think it might be helpful have your lawyer help you practice answering questions or being deposed.

Some lawyers are intimidating because of their aura of education, accomplishment or superiority, which they use in dealing with lawyers and non-lawyers alike. All professionals should be treated with respect, but then, almost everyone should be treated with respect. Don't defer to a lawyer just because of who they are. Don't give up rights or objectives important to you just because your lawyer intimates that he knows best. When your lawyer gives advice it should be well-defined and well-explained. In the end the decisions are still yours.

Remember that professionals are trained to help you solve specific kinds of problems. Legal professionals are trained and experienced in solving specific types of legal problems. Lawyers rely on clients for their living and you have the ability to choose the right lawyer and hold your lawyer responsible for delivering a good legal product.

Be respectful, focus on solving your legal problem and act professionally; but don't be intimidated by lawyers.

---

**Lawyer-Client Rule Number 3 . . . Page 35**

Ask "dumb" questions in a smart way. Be prepared with questions you want to ask. Document the answers. Respect the lawyer's time, but don't be afraid to ask a question.

---

Have the courage to ask questions. One of your lawyer's responsibilities is to keep you informed throughout the process. So ask questions and don't be concerned about asking ones that are dumb or that demonstrate your ignorance of the law and the legal system.

You aren't supposed to be knowledgeable about the law; that's why you hired a lawyer. But you still need to ask questions in a smart way. It can be frustrating for a lawyer to respond to questions that have already been answered in letters or reports sent to you. You'll soon be frustrated too when you realize that asking questions your lawyer has already answered is costing you more in hourly fees.

Make sure you read the reports and documents sent to you. You'll have questions about these documents, but a question about something specific in a report is better than questions that ask your lawyer to repeat the whole report. You may be able to do research yourself to find answers to your questions and some questions can reasonably be directed to associates or paralegals. Use e-mail for questions when you can, this gives your lawyer time to research or think about his response.

Take notes when you talk with your lawyer so you don't repeat questions you've forgotten the answer to. You can even ask your lawyer to send a short note summarizing your discussion. I always appreciated the chance to help educate my clients on complicated legal issues, but I did feel frustrated responding to the same questions over again or when it was clear that the client hadn't taken any time to review the reports or documents I'd already sent.

---

**Lawyer-Client Rule Number 4 . . . Page 37**

Take the time to find the best lawyer for you. Research, get recommendations and interview several lawyers. Don't hire the first lawyer you talk to unless time is limited and who you hire will have little impact on the outcome.

---

Unless they're sitting in jail cell and need legal help immediately most clients have time to find the right lawyer. Unfortunately, what usually happens is that you get a recommendation or see an advertisement and hire the first lawyer you talk to.

Just because a friend or family member knows a lawyer or goes to church with one does not mean that the lawyer is right for you or for your problem. A lawyer who handled a co-worker's divorce may be a great divorce lawyer, but that doesn't mean he should be your lawyer for a business or personal-injury matter.

Whenever possible, you should interview at least three lawyers. In some small towns this might not be feasible, but still make an effort to identify lawyers who handle your type of case and interview as many as you can. Be careful of hiring the first lawyer you talk to.

Often a prospective client will meet with a potential lawyer because they have no previous experience with lawyers to compare to they feel obligated to agree to a lawyer-client relationship and may even sign agreements to create a formal relationship, including an obligation to pay a fee.

Even if you like the lawyer, don't agree to hire him during the first interview. Go home and think about it away from the lawyer and his office. Meet with several other lawyers. Compare the offices and staff and get a sense of how different lawyers feel about your case.

Last, and most importantly, in addition to the lawyer interviewing you—make sure you are interviewing the lawyer. See Chapter 4 and the interview outline in Chapter 15 for examples of questions to ask. Find out how much experience your lawyer has in handling your type of problem. You want a sense of how well a lawyer listens and the way that he responds to your questions will help you decide whether you can work together for what might be years.

Be prepared with written questions. If you realize after the initial meeting or after interviewing another lawyer that you have additional questions, you can call the lawyer or send an e-mail. You are hiring a lawyer. That makes you an employer and requires you to take the steps necessary to hire the right one.

> **Lawyer-Client Rule Number 5 . . . Page 48**
> Stay focused on the legal problem and the best possible outcome. Don't get lost in the side battles or control expenses to the detriment of your result.

Don't rely on the legal system to solve all of your problems, to get revenge or to provide your retirement. Insist that your lawyer follow the ethical rules. Don't allow every dispute to become a major battle. Focus your strategy, your emotions and your resources on getting the result you need from the legal system.

Too many times I have seen clients get so wrapped up in the nuance and processes of the legal system that they seem to forget what the lawsuit is about. This is more common when the original case is about emotional issues—the breakup of a marriage or a business partnership. Or a claim for injuries, real or imagined. I've been in depositions and hearings where clients and lawyers are threatening to beat each other up. I've seen the devastating impact of bad decisions by clients and their lawyers because of bad feelings and uncontrolled emotions—because they lost sight of what the lawsuit was about and what was likely to happen if a jury resolved issues they couldn't negotiate.

Your lawyer should not just be an advocate, willing to spend all of your money to defend your honor or chase elusive revenge. Your lawyer should be a counselor who tells you that you can lose and sometimes that you're going to lose.

The other extreme is being so cheap that you lose far more than you have to because you aren't willing to hire the right lawyer or spend money on the resources that you need to win. Know what's at risk and don't be so careful with expenses that you lose the case. Listen to your lawyer and put yourself in the best position to prevail.

In the end, it's your responsibility to stay focused on the best possible result and keep your case on track, make sure that your money is being used wisely and to stop the side wars that are keeping you from your objective. Stay focused.

> **Lawyer-Client Rule Number 6 . . . Page 62**
>
> Always tell your lawyer the truth. Your lawyer needs to know the good and the bad facts. Your lawyer cannot tell anyone your secrets, but he needs to know all the facts.

A client who lies to his or her lawyer makes a serious mistake. One of the important reasons you hire a lawyer is for his counsel, but good counsel requires as much knowledge of the facts as possible.

Never lie to your lawyer. Communication with your lawyer is protected. Unless your lawyer doesn't want you to tell him everything—which sometimes happens in criminal cases—you need to share everything you know or believe about the case with him.

Don't try to impress your lawyer by bending the facts in a way you think will help your case. That's the lawyer's job!

> **Lawyer-Client Rule Number 7 . . . Page 82**
>
> Stay organized. You'll receive many documents throughout a case. If you allow them to get unorganized it will be difficult to get organized later and you won't be as informed as you need to be.

The key to staying on top of the legal problem and the process is to receive regular updates, be copied on important documents and keep the documents organized. See Chapter 11 for ideas and tips on staying organized.

Keep a working file that holds copies of important documents and reports, and organize the rest of the documents when you get them. Avoid letting letters and reports pile up in a box or in a drawer until the job of figuring out what you have becomes daunting and you give up before you start. Figure out a system, find a place to keep your case-related documents safe and use it when documents and reports arrive.

> **Lawyer-Client Rule Number 8 . . . Page 83**
> The lawyer advises and advocates. The client decides.

This is your legal problem. The legal problem that needs to be solved is your problem. You will have to live with the outcome, the verdict or the resolution. Your lawyer will have other clients, other legal battles and will continue to make a living representing clients with similar problems.

As a client, you have to take responsibility for your case. If you abandon the case to a lawyer then you'll have to be satisfied with the result, no matter what it is. And you'll get to pay the bill, no matter what that is.

When you take the time to hire a lawyer that you trust, who has expertise solving your type of problem you should let your lawyer do what he does best. But you have to take responsibility for managing the process, case and the result.

It takes a lot of time and work to manage a legal case. It takes effort to stay organized, to keep in communication and to be willing to ask the tough questions. Don't be afraid to ask stupid questions. Understand what is going on and make the tough decisions. Tough decisions need to focus on the results you want, so make sure that you use resources responsibly.

> **Lawyer-Client Rule Number 9 . . . Page 163**
> Listen to your lawyer. Regularly ignoring your lawyer's counsel will hurt your result and the lawyer-client relationship.

If you're making all of the tough decisions, what is your lawyer doing? Your lawyer is practicing law, researching, investigating and working the case towards your desired outcome. Hopefully your lawyer is also giving you advice on the merits, your options and strategy for moving the it forward. If you hired a good lawyer and you've told him what you're trying to accomplish—trust him to get you there.

Nothing destroys a professional relationship as fast as suspicion and contention. If you have issues with bills or how the case is being handled tell your lawyer right away. Don't let these issues drag on. If you want the case to go in another direction or to be resolved then make those decisions. If your lawyer objects because your decision or request violates an ethical rule, respect your lawyer. If he objects for what appears to be his own reasons and you can't trust him anymore, find another lawyer.

Define your objectives for the case. Make sure your expectations about billing, communication and decision making are clear and well documented. If your lawyer is working towards your objectives, and meeting your expectations than trust him.

# 15. Sample Letters and Forms

These sample letters provide a guide for you to document the legal process or communicate with your lawyer. When you actually write to your lawyer, make sure you take time to communicate your issues and circumstances rather just following these forms blindly.

## 15.1 Interview Outline

Date of Interview: _____

Lawyer: _____

Firm: _____

Size of Firm: _____

Lawyer Education: _____
_____

Past Work Experience (non-law experience and previous law employment or firms): _____
_____

Lawyer's Expertise (Focus of practice, types of cases and knowledge of law of your case): _____
_____

Lawyer's Past Cases like Yours: _____
_____
_____

Other Staff Members Who Will Be Working on Your File (Associates, Paralegals and Assistants): _____
_____
_____

Notes from Discussion of the Case:


Lawyer's Impressions of the Case:


Fees: _____
_____
_____

Retainer: $_____
Estimated Cost: $_____
Timeframe:


Follow-up Required:
1)
2)
3)


Your Impression of the Office: _____
_____


Your Impression of the Lawyer: _____
_____

## 15.2 Engagement Letter

This is a letter you send to the lawyer letting him know you've chosen him for representation. It can be sent via e-mail. Make sure that your letter reflects the actual terms and information you and your lawyer discussed.

For alternate billing arrangements (contingent fees, fixed fees, or other arrangements), you'll need to modify the letter. Your lawyer will probably prepare an agreement or documentation regarding the fees.

---

Dear [Lawyer],

This [letter/e-mail] is to confirm that I have retained you and your firm to represent me in [describe the nature of the problem or put in the name of the case]. *Examples—my dispute with my neighbor regarding the damage to our property, or, filing for a divorce from my spouse, or, the litigation filed against me, Jones vs. Smith.*

It is my understanding that you are able to represent me in this matter, that there are no conflicts of interest and that you have expertise and experience in handling legal problems like mine.

Your hourly rate for work done on this matter is [$150.00] an hour. You have indicated that [associate name], your associate, will also be working on this case and charges [$100.00] an hour and that your paralegals will also be billing for services at a rate of [$60] an hour.

You have indicated that you require a retainer fee of [$5,000.00]. Please let me know how this money should be paid. You will be holding this money in your client trust account until the end of this case when it will be returned to me.

I understand that it is hard to know the final cost of representing me in this matter, but you have estimated, based on your experience that the cost will be approximately [$15,000.00]. Please let me know as soon as possible if it becomes clear that the cost, including fees and expenses, will exceed this amount.

I would also like to be contacted in advance of any specific project or activity that will cost in excess of $1,000 so I am aware of what is going on and can authorize the expense.

I would like to be billed on a monthly basis, with a bill itemized in tenth-of-an-hour increments that includes descriptions of work performed.

My objective in this matter is [your issues, concerns and goal]. Examples—getting a cost-effective resolution to this dispute that allows me to build by home on the land we own, or, ending my marriage as quickly and efficiently as possible while ensuring a fair distribution of our assets. I would like to take advantage of any opportunity to seek a resolution that fits within the parameters we discussed.

I am committed to working with you in this matter. I am providing all of my contact information below but ask that you limit communication at my work.

> [Home Address]
>
> [Home Telephone]
>
> [Cell Telephone]
>
> [Work Name and Location]
>
> [Work Telephone]
>
> [E-mail Address]

I look forward to working with you. I very much appreciate your willingness to represent me. Please let me know what I need to do to help your representation be more effective.

Very Truly Yours,

Your New Client

## 15.3  Confirming Conversations and Decisions

This letter (or e-mail) is used to confirm when you have had a discussion with your lawyer regarding a specific matter and a decision has been made. The purpose is to make sure that both you and your lawyer are on the same page and that you have documentation of significant decisions.

Here are two examples.

---

Dear [Lawyer],

I appreciate the opportunity to talk this afternoon regarding the most recent bill I received for services rendered in month of June. As we discussed, I had several concerns about the total billed and specifically about several issues that I observed in the bill.

The first thing that we agreed was that there was an error with the hourly billing rate for your associate, [Associate's Name]. His time in June was billed at a rate of $150 an hour, instead of the agreed rate of $100.00 an hour. You agreed that this was an error, resulting in an immediate reduction in the amount of $1,400.00.

In addition, Mr. [Associate] spent 50 hours preparing a motion that I was unaware we needed to file. Because no one contacted me prior to starting a project of this size, resulting in over $5,000 in fees, you have agreed to reduce the cost of the time spent in this project by 20%. You agreed in a reduction of the bill from $10,460.00 to $6,368.00, which reflects the appropriate hourly rate for Mr. [Associate] and the discount in the time related to the motion project.

Thank you for working with me on these issues. I will make payment as soon as I receive the corrected bill.

Dear [Lawyer],

Thank you for calling me this afternoon. As we discussed, I am willing to accept the terms of the resolution to my litigation that you have so diligently negotiated.

My understanding of the negotiated settlement of this litigation is [terms of settlement]. If I am wrong about any of these points, please call me immediately.

I cannot tell you how much I appreciate your efforts and work to reach this resolution.

## 15.4 Status Report Outline

In longer, more complicated cases it can be a good idea to receive regular updates on the status. Below is an outline that can be used by your lawyer to prepare and update reports to you.

Remember that preparing reports takes time and costs money. The decision on getting status reports is yours, and in some cases, it can be a vital communication tool.

Even if you don't get a written report, this outline can help you discuss the case and important issues.

---

Status Report

Name of Case:

Lawyer Preparing Report:

Date of Report:

Parties:

Trial Date:

Status of Case:

Costs to Date:

Projected Future Costs:

*Facts and Issues:* Summary of the facts as they have been developed through the case and the issues that are being disputed.

*Witnesses:* Summary of who the witnesses are and what they will say.

*Evaluation:* Lawyer's evaluation of the case, the chance of success, and possible outcomes, including a discussion of the exposure to parties in money or chances of getting relief.

*Recommendations and Plan of Action:* Ask your lawyer to make recommendations on both future strategy and resolution. Ask him to put thought into what needs to happen to get the case prepared for the next step and possibly for trial.

## 15.5 Complaint/Issue Letter

This is a serious letter that should be sent when there is an unresolved issue. This is not the first step you take when a problem comes up, but a more formal communication of concerns. It expresses the need for immediate action by your lawyer. If you've consulted with another lawyer regarding the case he may be able to help you draft this letter.

---

Dear [Lawyer],

Over the past several weeks I have attempted to speak with you regarding the status of my case. It has been several months since we have talked or since I have received any meaningful communication. If there is no change in the status of my case, I can understand that there is little to report, but it is troubling to me as a client not to have any communication from my lawyer.

[Summarize the issues—billing, status reports, length of case or total cost of the matter] Example—It was my understanding that we would be close to a resolution of this litigation by the end of last year. Not only does the matter continue to drag on, but I feel that I'm not receiving the information I need to participate in my legal problem.

It is important that we talk. I need to understand the status of my case and understand your plan of action to resolve this matter. Please contact me before the end of the week, at least to set up a time for us to meet. If there is an issue or a problem with my case I need to know about it immediately.

I look forward to talking to you.

## 15.6 Replacement Letter

This is another serious communication. It should be in writing and done only when you mean it. Don't waste a lot of time or communication threatening to fire your lawyer. Try to resolve issues until you make a decision to change lawyers and have already found a replacement.

This is not a complicated letter, keep it short and sweet. Don't make a list of grievances and don't be insulting or personal. The focus should be on the orderly transfer of your file from one lawyer to another. Have your new lawyer review the letter before you send it.

---

Dear [Lawyer],

This letter is to inform you that I have made the decision to terminate our lawyer-client relationship. I have retained other counsel and ask that you cooperate with my new lawyer in the transfer of my case and materials.

The new lawyer for my case is [Lawyer's name] with the firm of [Firm]. His telephone number is [telephone]. He will contact you within the next several days to make arrangements for this transfer.

Thank you.

# 16   Sample Jury Instructions

These are a sample of the general instructions that explain the duties of the jurors and how the evidence is to be used by the jury as they reach a decision. In a trial these instructions are read to the jury after all of the evidence has been presented—at the very end of the trial. The judge reads them word for word and the instructions, along with the jury verdict form are given to the jury to be used during their deliberations.

General Instructions

1.1 INTRODUCTION

Members of the Jury:

Now that you have heard all of the evidence, it becomes my responsibility to instruct, or charge you, concerning the law that applies to this case. It is the judge's duty to consider, determine, and explain the rules of law that apply in a particular case. It is the jury's responsibility and duty to consider and determine the facts of the case—that is, what the jury believes to be the true facts from among all of the evidence in the case. I have no right to tell you which facts are established by the testimony and any exhibits. You, and only you, are the judges of the facts.

1.2 DUTY TO FOLLOW INSTRUCTIONS

It is your duty as jurors to accept and follow the law as contained in these instructions and to apply that law to the facts that you believe have been proved from all of the evidence in the case. Each instruction is as important as any other. You are not to single out one statement or instruction alone as stating the law and ignore the other instructions or parts of instructions. You are to consider and apply these instructions together as a whole, and you are to regard each instruction in the light of all others.

Any personal opinion which you, or any of you, may have as to facts not established by the evidence in this case cannot properly be considered by you as a basis for your verdict. As individuals, you may believe that certain facts existed, but as jurors sworn to try this case and to render a true verdict on the law and the evidence, you can act only upon the evidence which has been properly introduced to you at this trial. You cannot speculate as to what may have happened in the absence of evidence on a given point. If you have any personal opinion as to what the law is, or ought to be, you must put that opinion aside and accept and apply the law as it is.

### 1.3 SYMPATHY

In performing your duties as jurors, you must not permit yourself to be influenced or swayed by sympathy, bias, prejudice, or favor to any party. All parties expect that you will carefully and impartially consider all of the evidence, accept and follow the law as contained in these instructions, and reach a just verdict, regardless of the consequences.

### 1.4 NATURAL PERSONS AND CORPORATE CITIZENS

You should consider and decide this case as an action between persons of equal standing in the community, of equal worth, and holding the same or similar stations in life. A corporation is entitled to the same fair trial at your hands as a private individual. All persons, including corporations, stand equal before the law, and are to be dealt with as equals in a court of justice.

### 1.5 CONSIDERATION OF THE EVIDENCE

You are to determine the facts of this case from the evidence alone. The "evidence" in the case always consists of the sworn testimony of all the witnesses, whether the witness appeared in person or by deposition, regardless of who may have called the witness, and all exhibits received in evidence, regardless of who may have produced them. Accordingly, during your deliberations, you should carefully consider the testimony of each and every witness and all exhibits.

### 1.6 DIRECT AND CIRCUMSTANTIAL EVIDENCE

There are, generally speaking, two types of evidence from which a jury may properly find the truth as to the facts of the case. One is direct evidence, such as the testimony of an eyewitness. The other is indirect or circumstantial evidence—the proof of a chain of circumstances pointing to the existence or non-existence of certain facts. As a general rule, the law makes no distinction between direct and circumstantial evidence, but simply requires that the jury find the facts in accordance with all of the evidence in this case, both direct and circumstantial.

### 1.7 FACTS AND INFERENCES

You are to consider only the evidence presented, and you may not guess or speculate as to the existence of any facts in this case. But in your consideration of the evidence, you are not limited to the bald statements of the witnesses. On the contrary, you are permitted to draw reasonable inferences that seem justified in the light of your own experiences from the facts you find have been proved. Inferences are deductions or conclusion which reason and common sense lead the jury to draw from facts that have been established by the evidence in the case.

1.8 ARGUMENTS AND STIPULATIONS

Nothing I have said or done at any time during this trial shall be considered by you as evidence of any fact, or as an indication that I have any opinion concerning any fact, the credibility of the witnesses, or the weight of the evidence.

You should entirely disregard questions and exhibits to which an objection was sustained, or answers or exhibits that I have ordered stricken from the evidence. It is not the jury's job to determine the admissibility or validity of an exhibit or other testimony. Do not draw any conclusions or speculations about why certain testimony or other evidence was excluded or admitted.

Nothing said or done by the attorneys is to be considered by you as evidence of fact. Opening statements and final arguments are intended to help you to understand the evidence and apply the law, but they are not evidence.

Anything you may have seen or heard outside the courtroom is not evidence, and must be entirely disregarded.

1.9 CREDIBILITY OF WITNESSES

In saying that you must consider all of the evidence, I do not mean that you must accept all of the evidence as true or accurate. You, as jurors, are the sole judges of the *credibility of the witnesses* and the *weight of the evidence*.

The *credibility of a witness* means the truthfulness or lack of truthfulness of the witness. The *weight of the evidence* means the extent to which you are—or are not—convinced by the evidence. You should carefully scrutinize the testimony given, the circumstances under which the witness has testified, and every matter in evidence which tends to indicate whether the witness is worthy of belief.

Inconsistencies or discrepancies in the testimony of a witness, or between the testimonies of differing witnesses, should be considered by you, and may or may not cause you to discredit such testimony. Two or more persons witnessing an incident may see or hear it differently. Innocent mis-recollection—like failure of recollection—is not an uncommon experience. In weighing their effect, you should consider whether the inconsistencies or discrepancies pertain to a matter of importance, or an unimportant detail, and whether the discrepancy or inconsistency results from innocent error or willful falsehood.

The number of witnesses testifying on one side or the other of an issue is not alone the test of the credibility of the witnesses and the weight of the evidence. If warranted by the evidence, you may believe one witness against a number of witnesses testifying differently.

The tests are: How truthful is the witness and how convincing is his or her evidence, and which witnesses and which evidence appeals to your minds as being most accurate and otherwise trustworthy in the light of all the evidence and circumstances shown.

In determining the credit and weight that you will give to the testimony of any witness who has testified before you, you may consider if found by you from the evidence:

(1) His or her good memory or lack of memory;

(2) The witness's interest, or lack of interest, in the outcome of the trial;

(3) The witness's relationship to any of the parties or other witnesses;

(4) His or her demeanor and manner of testifying;

(5) His or her opportunity and means or lack of opportunity, and means to know the things about which he or she testified;

(6) The reasonableness, or unreasonableness of his or her testimony;

(7) His or her apparent fairness, or lack of fairness;

(8) The intelligence, or lack of intelligence, of the witness;

(9) The bias, prejudice, hostility, friendliness or unfriendliness of the witness for or against any of the parties;

(10) Contradictory statements of any witness, if you believe the witness made any statements contradictory to his or her testimony.

Understand, however, that you may not use statements you determine to be contradictory to establish the truth of such statements, unless the statements are made under oath in the court room.

(11)     Witnesses' acts that you believe contradict their testimony;

From these considerations, and all other conditions and circumstances appearing from the evidence, you may give to the testimony of the witness such credit and weight as you believe it is entitled to receive.

If you believe that any witness in this case has knowingly testified falsely as to any material fact, after considering and weighing the testimony of such witness, you may disregard the whole of the testimony of the witness, or give it whatever weight and credit you believe the testimony is entitled to receive.

### 1.10 EXPERT WITNESSES—OPINIONS

Ordinarily, witnesses are not permitted to testify as to opinions or conclusions. However, the rules of evidence provide that if scientific, technical, or other specialized knowledge might assist the jury in understanding the evidence or in determining a fact in issue, a witness qualified as an expert by knowledge, skill, experience, training or education, may testify and state his opinion concerning such matters and may state the reasons for the opinion.

You should consider each expert opinion received in evidence in this case, and the reasons given in support of the opinion, and give it whatever weight you think it deserves. In determining the weight to be given to the opinion of an expert, you should consider the education, training and experience of the expert, the basis for the opinion, the confidence of the witness, the reasons and reasoning stated by the witness, the opinions of other similar witnesses on the same matters, and the rules generally applicable to other witnesses in this case.

If you should decide that the opinion of an expert witness is not based upon sufficient education and/or experience, or if you should conclude that the reasons given in support of the opinion are not sound, or merely speculative, or that the opinion is outweighed by other evidence, then you may disregard the opinion entirely, or give it such weight as you find it deserves.

## 1.11 BURDEN OF PROOF

The burden of proof is on the plaintiff in a civil action such as this to prove each and every essential element of his or her claim by a preponderance of the evidence. If the proof should fail to establish any element of the plaintiff's claim by a preponderance of the evidence in the case, or if the defendant's evidence outweighs the plaintiff's, or if the evidence is evenly balanced in the case, the jury should find for the defendant as to that claim.

*To establish by a preponderance of the evidence* means to prove that something is more likely so than not so. In other words, a preponderance of the evidence means a body of evidence has more convincing force than the evidence that opposed it, and evidence that produces a belief in your mind that what a party is trying to prove is more likely true than not true.

While the burden is on the plaintiff to prove his claim by a preponderance of the evidence, this rule does not require proof to an absolute certainty, since proof to an absolute certainty is seldom possible in any case. In a civil case, as opposed to criminal cases, it is proper to find that the plaintiff has succeeded in carrying the burden of proof if you believe that the evidence of the plaintiff outweighs that of the defendant even in the slightest degree, after considering all the evidence in the case.

## 1.12 IMPEACHMENT

A witness may be discredited or *impeached* by contradictory evidence, by showing that he or she testified falsely concerning a material matter, or by evidence that at some other time a witness has said or done something, or has failed to say or do something, that is inconsistent with the witness's present testimony.

If you believe that any person testifying in this case has knowingly testified falsely to any material fact, you may believe such parts of their testimony as you believe to be true and reject such parts as you believe to be false, or you may refuse to believe any part of such testimony. It is for you to determine, from all the testimony taken and all the circumstances surrounding this case, which witnesses have testified truthfully and which ones, if any, have testified falsely.

## 1.13 VIDEO TESTIMONY

During the trial of this case, certain testimony has been presented to you by way of a deposition on a video recording played on a television set, which consisted of sworn recorded answers to questions asked of the witness in advance of this trial by one or more of the attorneys for the parties in this case. The testimony of a witness who, for some reason cannot be present to testify in person from the witness stand, may be presented under oath on a video recording played on a television set. Such testimony is entitled to the same consideration, credibility, and weight by the jury as if the witness had been present and had testified from the witness stand.

## 1.14 NEGLIGENCE

In determining the primary question before you, it will be necessary to know and understand what is meant by *negligence, contributory negligence, proximate cause,* and *assumption of risk.*

*Negligence* is the failure to exercise ordinary care. Ordinary care is that kind and degree of care or caution which an ordinary prudent and careful person would exercise under the same or similar circumstances.

Negligence is doing something a reasonably prudent person would not do in the same or similar circumstances, or the failing or refusing to do something a reasonably prudent persons would have done in the same, or similar circumstance. Negligence cannot be presumed, but must be proven.

*Contributory negligence* means negligence of the plaintiff, which, together with negligence of the defendant, proximately caused the accident. Where contributory negligence is charged by a party, the contributory negligence charged must be proven by the party asserting it by a preponderance of the evidence.

*The proximate cause* of an event is the negligent act contributing to the accident, without which the accident would not have occurred. The proximate cause of an event is that cause which, in actual sequence, unbroken by any independent cause, produces an event, and without which, the event would not have occurred.

*Assumption of risk* means that the plaintiff, knowing full well the hazards involved, failed to take precautions to protect himself from those known or reasonably to be expected hazards.

## 1.15 COMPARATIVE NEGLIGENCE

Under the law of comparative negligence as adopted the state, a plaintiff is barred from recovery if his negligence equals or exceeds 50 percent of the total negligence of all parties to the accident, which total negligence our law sets at 100 percent.

If you find from a preponderance of the evidence that the defendant was guilty of negligence that proximately contributed to the damages incurred by the plaintiff, and you further find from a preponderance of the evidence that the plaintiff was guilty of negligence which proximately caused his damages, but that his negligence was not greater than 50 percent of the total negligence, then you will determine the percentage of the plaintiff's negligence compared to the total negligence of all parties, which our law expresses at 100 percent. You will then also determine total damages of the plaintiff without regard to his percentage or degree of negligence.

## 1.16 JUROR RESPONSIBILITY

Your part in the administration of justice is very important. The parties in this case have come into this court for a trial on issues that have developed and exist between them. It is our duty—mine as judge, and yours as jurors—to see that all parties get a full and fair trial. You have been chosen and sworn as jurors to try the issues of fact presented in this case. You are to perform this duty without bias or prejudice to any party. The law does not permit jurors to be governed by conjecture, surmise, speculation, prejudice, or public opinion in these cases. The parties to this action rightfully expect that you will carefully and impartially consider all the evidence in the case and that you will carefully follow the law as stated to you by the Court.

Remember at all times that you are not partisans. You are judges—judges of fact. Your sole interest is to seek the truth from the evidence of the case.

You are to answer the questions on the jury verdict form solely upon the evidence received at this trial. You are to be guided by the court's instructions and your own sound judgment in considering the evidence in this case and in answering these questions.

After the closing arguments, this case is ready to be submitted to you for your serious deliberations. You will consider the case fairly, honestly, impartially, and in light of reason and common sense, and you will give each question on the verdict form your careful and conscientious consideration. Let your verdict speak the truth, whatever that truth may be.

## 1.17 MECHANICS OF DELIBERATION

This case will now be submitted to you with a verdict form, which is a series of questions. Your duty will be discharged by responding to the ones you deem appropriate based on the evidence and the court's instructions. You will complete your work when you return the verdict form to the court. It thereupon becomes the court's duty to direct judgment according to law and according to the facts as you have found them.

Upon retiring to your jury room, you should first select one of your number to act as a foreperson who will preside over your deliberations and will be your spokesperson here in court.

You will take the verdict form to your jury room, and when you have reached unanimous agreement as to the verdict, you will have your foreperson fill it out, date and sign it, and return it to the courtroom.

Your verdict must represent the considered judgment of each juror. In order to return a verdict, it is necessary that each juror agree to it. In other words, your verdict must be unanimous.

If you should desire to communicate with the court during the deliberations, please reduce your message to writing signed by the foreperson and pass the note to the bailiff, who will bring it to my attention. I will then respond as promptly as possible, either in writing or by having you returned to the courtroom so that I can address you orally. I caution you, however, that any message or question you might send should never state or specify how the jury stands, numerically or otherwise.

www.ingramcontent.com/pod-product-compliance
Lightning Source LLC
Chambersburg PA
CBHW061505180526
45171CB00001B/45